# SECRETS OF CENTRAL LONDON'S SQUARES

Alan Brooke & David Brandon



AMBERLEY

First published 2016

Amberley Publishing
The Hill, Stroud, Gloucestershire, GL5 4EP
www.amberley-books.com



ISBN 978 1 4456 5664 9 (print)
ISBN 978 1 4456 5665 6 (ebook)



British Library Cataloguing in Publication Data.
A catalogue record for this book is available from the British Library.

Typesetting by Amberley Publishing.
Printed in Great Britain.

# Introduction

A distinguishing feature of London is its squares. They are a form of architecture and town planning not exactly unique to the metropolis but never fully exploited in other cities –although it could be said that Bath, Edinburgh and Liverpool all made some use of the concept.

The archetype of the London square draws on the high point of its development in the early nineteenth century. We think of uniform and surrounded terraces that possess a certain self-conscious grandeur and a sense of propriety. We imagine enclosed gardens in the centre for recreation and for the love of nature that favoured and affluent residents upheld. This is more an ideal than a reality since uniformity of style around the sides of a square was rarely achieved even in what, at first sight, is the perceived perfection of Bedford Square. The grandest squares were largely in estates whose ground landlords were the Russell, Grosvenor, Portman and Cavendish-Bentinck families or their associates.

The London square has to be seen as an evolving historical and architectural phenomenon. Its origin probably lies in the work of Inigo Jones in Covent Garden in 1631–39 on land then owned by the Earls of Bedford and of which very few traces still exist. Asked to describe a 'typical' London square, it is likely that most people would describe it as being of the eighteenth-century Georgian period. However, many squares were built during the Victorian era – notably between 1840 and 1880 – in districts such as Kensington, Paddington and Islington. They were an architectural anachronism because they continued to be built in what can loosely be described as the Georgian style. After that, the building of squares fell away rapidly, as indeed did the associated grand terraced houses. Sporadic and less grandiose examples have been built since then, the most notable of which is Courtenay Square in Kennington, south of the Thames and built in 1913.

The earlier squares were paved and largely of open access, which made them less exclusive. The private enclosed garden in the centre of a square emerged as a conscious attempt to safeguard the existence of at least some open space as London expanded in the seventeenth and eighteenth centuries and especially the nineteenth century – even if the resulting 'green' amenity was only available to a small privileged elite. It was an early form of 'privatisation' in this case and it accentuated the class differences in society where there were enclaves given over almost exclusively to the enjoyment of the very rich. They were a clear statement of an extremely unequal society.

As the nineteenth century wore on, many resented the social privilege of these exclusive gated spaces. The closed or private garden squares had few, if any, occupants. Those that had open access drew huge numbers of visitors, clearly enjoying, respecting and appreciating the space and the surroundings.

George Orwell, writing in 1944, felt strongly about the exclusive nature of the squares:

> [T]he railings are returning in one London square after another ... So the lawful denizens of the squares can make use of their treasured keys again, and the children

> of the poor can be kept out. When the railings round the parks and squares were removed, the object was partly to accumulate scrap-iron, but the removal was also felt to be a democratic gesture. Many more green spaces were now open to the public, and you could stay in the parks till all hours instead of being hounded out at closing times by grim-faced keepers. The parks were improved out of recognition by being laid open, acquiring a friendly, almost rural look that they had never had before.
>
> *As I Please*, 1943–45

Most squares did their duty in the Second World War – and not just in giving up their iron rails. Belgrave Square became a tank park, St James's Square was dug up and used for vegetable growing, and air-raid shelters were built in Soho and Manchester squares.

Clearly, the squares are not actually square-shaped and not all are even rectangular. Some are large enough to have sizeable buildings such as churches in the centre (Smith Square, for example) and others have such little space in the middle that they are really just wide streets. Some, like Charterhouse Square, are virtually formless. There are squares, such as Park Square in Regent's Park, that have one side open to a main road with the other sides being built up.

Many of the squares display statuary. The desire to commemorate those who have predeceased us, especially if they have been notable in some way, is seemingly a strong one. The squares of London contain huge numbers of statues of the 'great and the good' and others who, frankly, as a modern wit has said, were celebrities known only for being well known with any genuine merit being far from obvious. Senior officers of the armed forces, monarchs and politicians are well to the fore, and scientists and others who may have improved the human lot less so. Sometimes, a statue may be an object of ridicule when pigeons, gulls or other birds perch on the stony cocked hat of an admiral of the fleet or do their business on the head of a politician. In the case of the latter, this may be symbolic justice.

A word of mention must go to London's plane trees, which account for over half of the city's tree population and are in evidence in many of the gardens of the squares covered in this book. These distinctive trees were formed by hybridisation in the seventeenth century and it is claimed that this process took place in Spain, but it could also have been in Vauxhall Gardens. They were planted mainly in London from the nineteenth century when population expansion forced greater urban planning. Inspired by the plane-lined boulevards built in Paris from around 1850, the tree flourished in London due to its hardy characteristics. Berkeley Square, which has around thirty, planted in 1789, is a particularly good place to view them.

This book is not intended to be a comprehensive coverage of all those spaces in Westminster or Bloomsbury that could, in the most liberal terms, be described as 'squares' – that would require a far greater undertaking. Rather, this book draws attention to the unusual, the quirky and the curious, as well as familiar features of selected squares. It also looks at aspects of their past and of what can be seen today, including some of the people who lived in these places. Some squares have an abundance of features and proved more favourable for photographic opportunities than others. Visiting these fascinating public spaces is a great pleasure and provides many unexpected discoveries.

# The Squares of Westminster

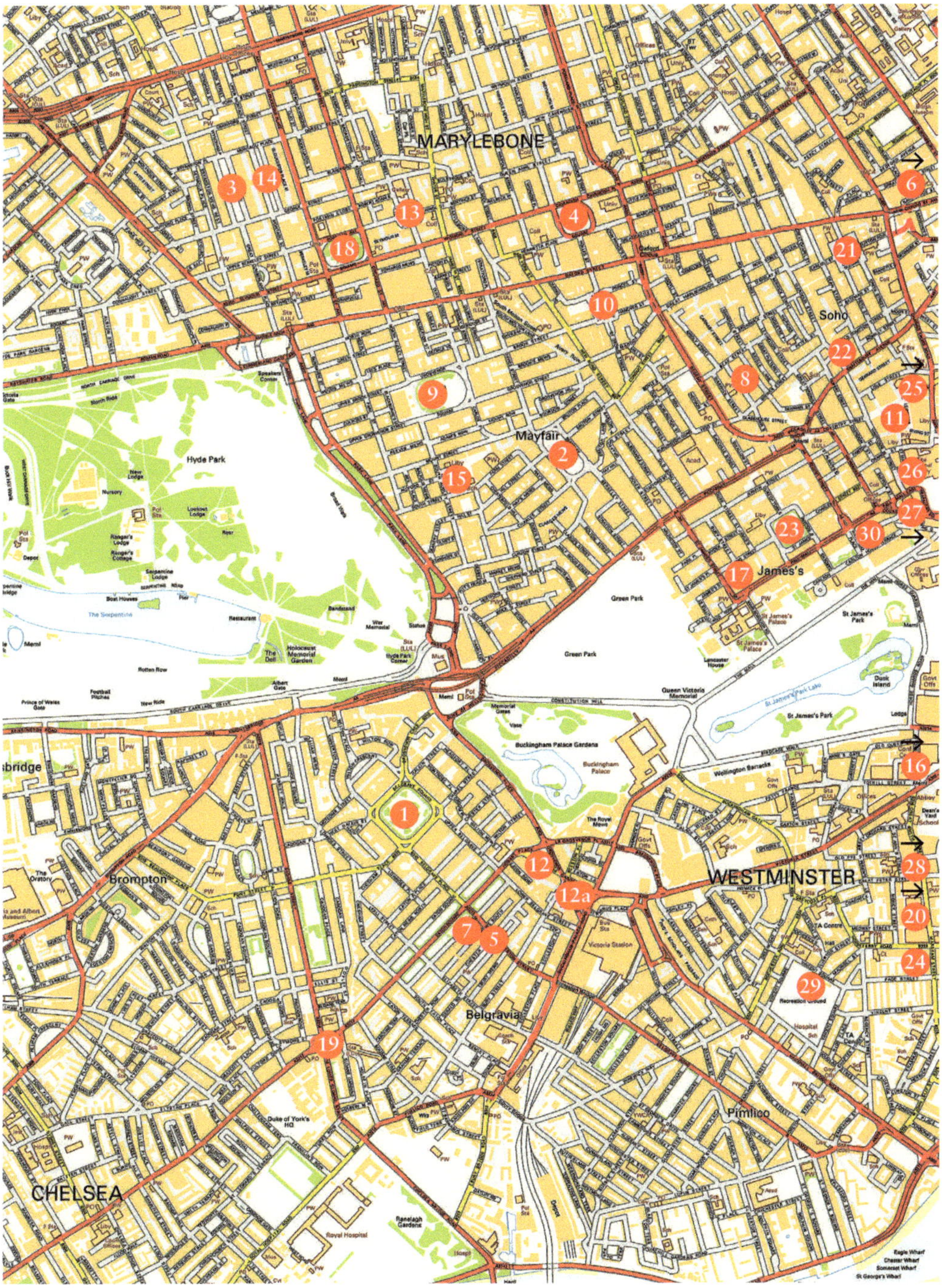

# 1. Belgrave Square

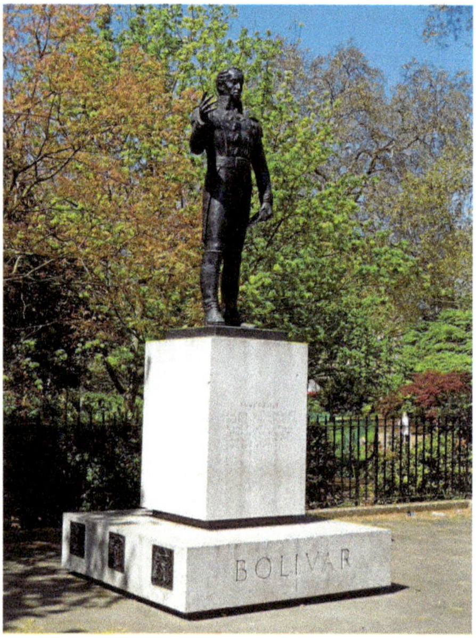


The statue of Simon Bolivar in Belgrave Square.

Belgrave Square is situated to the north-west of Victoria Tube Station and east of Knightsbridge Station. The square was completed in 1845 – although some say 1837 – on land previously used for pasture and market gardening. The land has been owned by the Grosvenor family since the seventeenth century.

Belgrave, from which it derives its name, is a small settlement on the Grosvenor family's estate near Chester. It is at the heart of the fashionable and affluent part of London known as Belgravia. It was, and remains, one of London's most prestigious squares and architecturally is probably the grandest. There are a number of embassies and residences for many countries, including Bahrain, Romania, Spain, Germany and Ghana (High Commission).

Before building development started, the area sometimes known as 'Five Fields' was notorious as a place for duelling and also for robberies during the hours of darkness. It had the advantage of being both close to London, with plenty of potential victims, and yet on the edge of countryside offering malefactors plenty of hiding places.

The square was laid out by the successful builder and property developer Thomas Cubitt (1788–1853). Even in these early days of property speculation there were risks attached and Cubitt decided to test the temperature by building a show house. He then only erected further buildings for which he knew he had firm offers. Cubitt worked with the architect George Basevi (1794–1845) until the latter fell to his death while working at Ely Cathedral. Basevi was a fashionable architect who worked mostly in the classical style and his best-known work is probably the Fitzwilliam Museum in Cambridge. He signed his name on the side of the portico of No. 37 Belgrave Square.

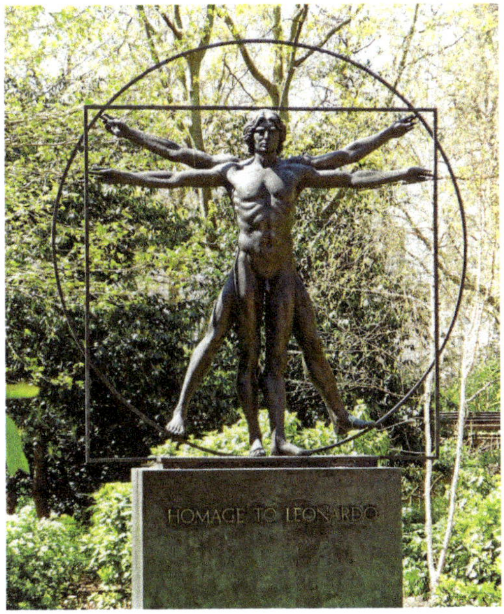


The *Homage to Leonardo* sculpture.

In the past, there were many aristocratic, fashionable or wealthy occupants of the square but the majority of its buildings are now offices or embassies. Henry 'Chips' Channon (1897–1958) resided at No. 5. He was born in the United States but moved to Britain in 1920. Immensely wealthy, he became virulently anti-American and anti-Communist. Described as an 'insufferable snob', he was a Conservative politician, author, diarist and socialite who managed to insinuate himself into Britain's inner political circles without it actually ever being very obvious what talent he had to offer. It is rumoured that large parts of his diaries have never been published and that they contained many revelations about the dissolute activities of society's so-called 'high and mighty'. Those in high places were understandably anxious to propitiate him and this may help to explain the social power he enjoyed.

On the wall of the Norwegian Embassy at No. 25 are two reliefs in Coade Stone depicting cherubs. A plaque reads, 'In 1776 these two Coade Stone reliefs were affixed to the Danish–Norwegian consulate in Wellclose Square, Stepney. In 1968 the reliefs were erected on this embassy by courtesy of the Greater London Council.' Coade Stone is an artificial terracotta which is largely weatherproof and which has been used extensively on grand buildings and for statues. It was manufactured at Lambeth between 1720 and 1840.

The coronation of Elizabeth II took place on 2 June 1953 and was planned by a team led by the Earl Marshal of England. This was a hereditary title then held by the 16th Duke of Norfolk. This dignitary at the time resided at No. 14. He was known to be an effective and efficient organiser but was, notoriously, a man of few words who disliked social gatherings. It is said that at a particular dinner party, he attempted to engage the lady next to him with this blunt opening gambit, 'Now, I have only two topics of conversation: cricket and drains. Choose.'

The gardens in Belgrave Square are private and retain some of their original character. They contain a number of plane trees that were planted when the gardens were initially laid out.

Among the statuary in the garden is one commemorating Simon Bolivar (1783–1830). Part of the inscription states, '… the liberator of Venezuela, Colombia, Ecuador, Peru and Panama … erected on behalf of the countries liberated and founded by Simon Bolivar'. The plinth contains Bolivar's own words: 'I am convinced that England alone is capable of protecting the world's precious rights as she is great, glorious and wise.' This statue was unveiled in 1974 by the then Foreign Secretary James Callaghan. Ironically, Bolivar died at a time when Britain was setting about creating the largest empire in history.

There is a sculpture in the gardens (which can be viewed from outside) entitled *Homage to Leonardo* by Enzo Plazzotta. The statue was completed posthumously by Plazzotta's assistant Mark Holloway in 1982 and was installed in 1984.

**Nearest tube:** Hyde Park Corner, Knightsbridge, Victoria.

## 2. Berkeley Square

Berkeley Square is located in Mayfair, north of Green Park Tube Station. This famous Mayfair Square, which has been memorialised in both song and film, originates from 1696 and was named after John, Lord Berkeley of Stratton.

In 1660, the 1st Baron Berkeley acquired land to the north of Piccadilly and built Berkeley House. In 1696, the 3rd Lord Berkeley sold the house to the Duke of Devonshire, on condition that Lord Berkeley protected the northward view by agreeing not to build on his land to the north. After Berkeley House burned down in 1733, some very grand properties were built on three sides of the oblong 'square'. The first houses to define the square were constructed around 1738 on the east side; the west side was finished by 1745. The present layout of the square dates from 1766. Lansdowne House is on the south side and was designed by Robert Adam around 1762. Since 1935, it has been the home of the Lansdowne Club.

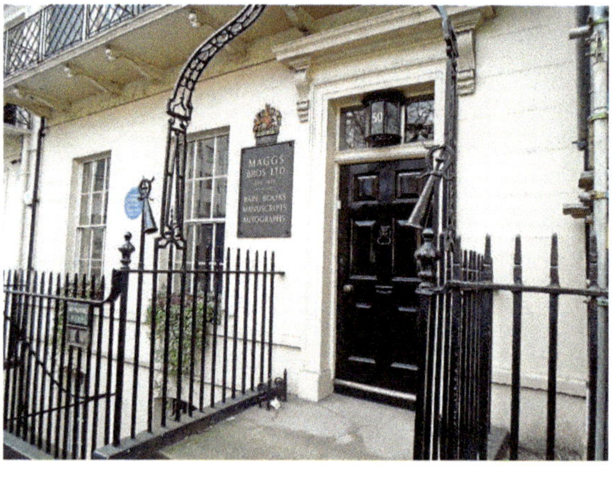

Maggs antiquarian bookshop in Berkeley Square – also a famous haunted house. Note the link extinguishers and shoe scraper.

During the twentieth century, much of the Georgian development was destroyed, notably on the east side, and replaced by car showrooms and office blocks. It is on the west side that glimpses of the original setting can be seen. The architectural historian Nikolaus Pevsner (1902–83) described No. 44, a Grade I-listed building, as 'the best terraced house in London'. It is now home to the Clermont Club, a private gaming club.

When Harry Gordon Selfridge, the successful American retail magnate, sold his Chicago department store for a large profit, he decided to bring his American shopping know-how to Britain. In 1909, he opened his modern flagship store, Selfridge's, in Oxford Street and it was an immediate success. He is attributed with coining the phrase 'Only – Shopping Days until Christmas' and 'The customer is always right.' Selfridge and his family eventually moved to a suite of rooms near Berkeley Square, No. 9 Fitzmaurice Place (south end), where they lived between 1921 and 1929. The building was restored in 2000 and a blue plaque was placed on the outside of the building to commemorate Harry Gordon Selfridge. Nearby is Charles Street where Winston Churchill lived, at No. 48, as a child (1874–79).

Berkeley Square boasts a number of distinguished residents including former Prime Minister George Canning (1770–1827), who served for only 119 days, the shortest tenure of any British prime minister. He resided at No. 50. Lord Robert Clive (1725–1774), one of the key figures in the creation of British India, lived at No. 45.

The square provided the residences for a number of famous fictional characters. No. 15 Berkeley Street appears in print as Bertie Wooster's flat (his creator, P. G. Wodehouse, lived there for a short time in 1922). Harry Flashman, the nasty bully of Tom Brown and anti-hero of the *Flashman Papers*, had a marital home here with his wife Elspeth.

No. 50 Berkeley Square is reputed to be one of the most haunted houses in Britain. Its ghostly sightings have included a little girl, a young woman and a grotesque man with a gaping mouth. A number of deaths have been attributed to the house after people stayed the night in the 'haunted' room. However, no unusual phenomena have been reported since the Maggs Brothers, antiquarian book dealers, bought the house in 1937.

More visibly interesting are the foot scraper and link extinguishers that can be seen outside the door of No. 50. There are also other extinguishers at Nos 43, 44 and Nos 46–49. No. 43 Berkeley Square also has a gaslight above the door. Before public lights were available, a link-boy (usually a poor street urchin) would, for a small fee, light the way for those wanting to find their way around the London streets. The torch was made from the dried pith of a rush plant dipped in fat or grease. Many houses had torch extinguishers on their gates.

Features to look out for in the gardens include the centrepiece which is a (now disused) pump house built in 1800. It is a Grade II-listed structure and features a chinoiserie roof and a veranda supported by slim iron pillars. There is also a sculptural fountain named *Woman of Samaria*, a nymph pouring water from a vase into a basin that dates from 1858 by Alexander Munro, a Pre-Raphaelite sculptor. To the north-west stands two traditional (functioning) London red phone boxes. Nearby on the corner of Hay's Mews and Charles Street is the unusually named pub, I Am the Only Running Footman, originally built in 1749 and rebuilt in 1937. The pub was frequented by the footmen who were in service to the households of Mayfair and one footman bought the pub and renamed it after himself. Sadly the pub closed in 2016.

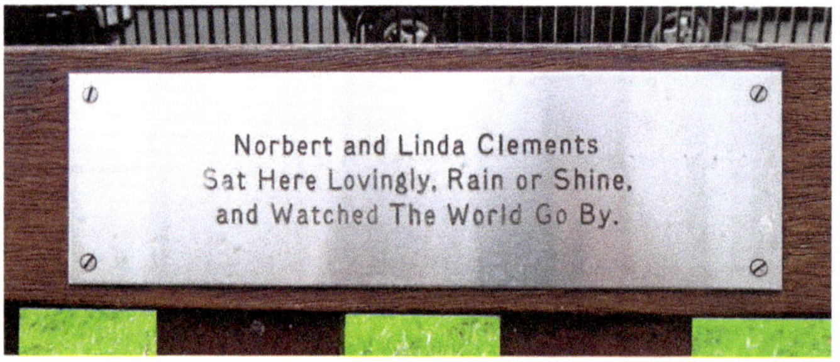


One of many benches with personal inscriptions in Berkeley Square Gardens.

An important feature of the gardens are the surrounding plane trees, of which around thirty were planted in 1789 and have the distinction of being among some of the oldest in Central London. In 2008, the 6-foot-wide tree in Berkeley Square emerged as the most valuable in the capital, estimated at £750,000.

Berkeley Square certainly has its romantic associations. The song, 'A Nightingale Sang in Berkeley Square' (1940), written by Eric Maschwitz with music by Manning Sherwin, quickly became a wartime favourite. The song concerns the magic of the meeting of two lovers and this is reflected in the lyrics, although the nightingale reference probably owes more to poetic licence than fact.

More visible signs of meetings and dedications of love can be seen in the brass inscriptions on many of the benches as well as a number of references to the nightingale. For example, 'A nightingale sang in Berkeley Square and in all our lives …' Other inscriptions reflect on those who sat here lovingly, come rain or shine, and watched the world go by, others who rekindled their love after thirty years, or Thomas J. Johnston of San Francisco who visited these gardens as a commander in the US Navy during the Normandy Landings; the dedications reflect a very moving but particular moment in people's lives and the extent to which the gardens played a part.

**Nearest tube:** Green Park.

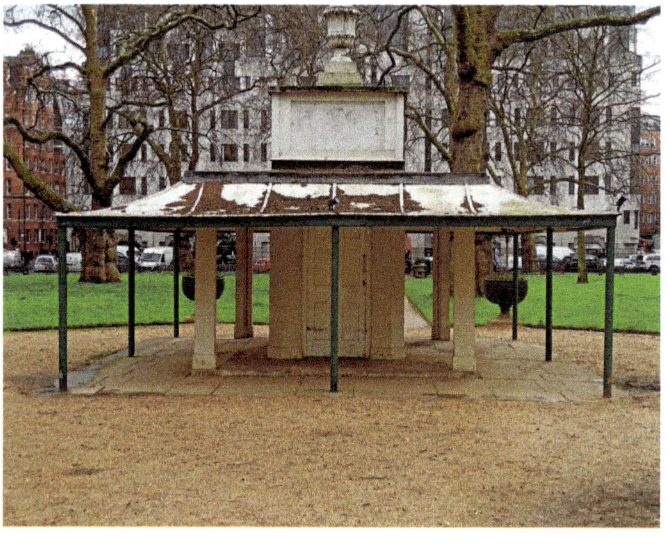

Pump House Gazebo, Berkeley Square Gardens.

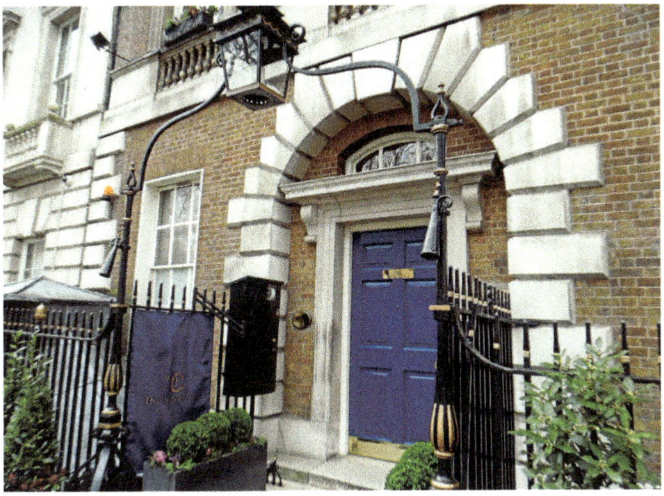

Nikolaus Pevsner described No. 44 Berkeley Square as 'the best terraced house in London'.

# 3. Bryanston Square

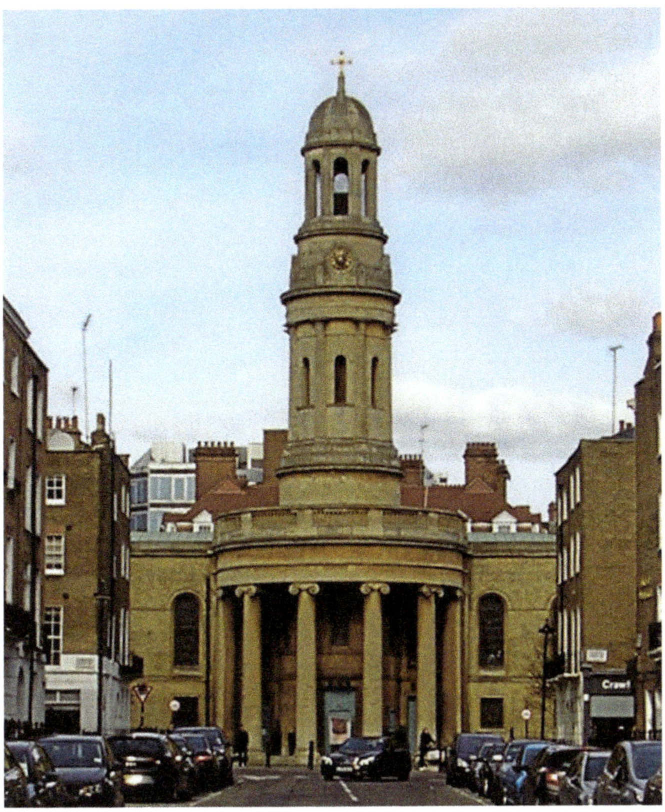

Bryanston Square looking north up Wyndham Place to St Mary's Church.

Bryanston Square is a long rectangular terraced square in Marylebone and is located north of Marble Arch Tube Station. The square has a pleasant green centre which is reserved for the use of residents.

The square was named after its founder Henry William Portman's home village of Bryanston in Dorset and the square was built as part of the Portman estate between 1810 and 1815 along with Montagu Square to the east. In the 1844 publication of *London in Six Volumes*, Charles Knight unkindly described both squares as 'twin deformities ... long narrow strips of ground, fenced in by two monotonous rows of flat houses'.

At the south end of the garden is a Grade II-listed memorial fountain with a heaped rock rubble base and shell basin erected in 1862. It was dedicated to William Pitt Byrne who was the owner and editor of *The Morning Post*, which later merged with the *Daily Telegraph* in 1937. At the opposite end of the garden is an ornamental cast-iron water pump in the form of a Doric column that dates from the early nineteenth century.

The original iron railings around the gardens were removed during the Second World War but new railings were restored in 1980. The gardens contain thirty-four London plane trees as well as cherry, lilac, laburnum, false acacia and Japanese maple trees.

The most notable landmark is the Grade I-listed St Mary's Church, Wyndham Place, built between 1821 and 1824. It provides a fine feature at the end of the formal vista through Bryanston Square.

The artist John Millais moved to Bryanston Square in 1860 and Wallis Simpson, the future wife of Edward VIII, Duke of Windsor, lived there just before Edward's abdication in December 1936. Appropriately, Bryanston Square was the address of Mr March in C. P. Snow's *The Conscience of the Rich* (1958).

**Nearest tube:** Marble Arch.

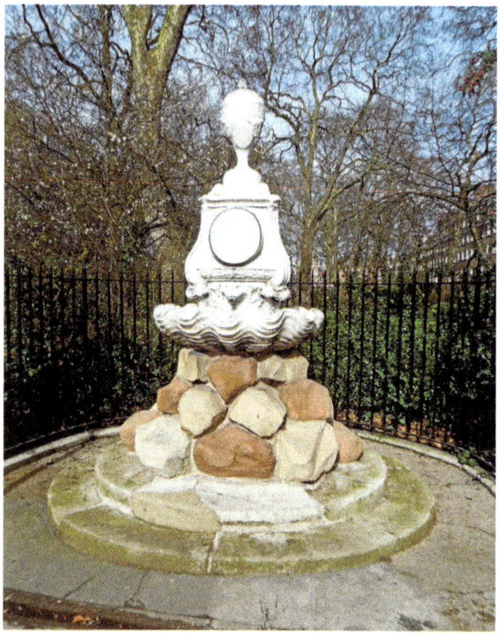

The memorial fountain to William Pitt Byrne in Bryanston Square.

# 4. Cavendish Square

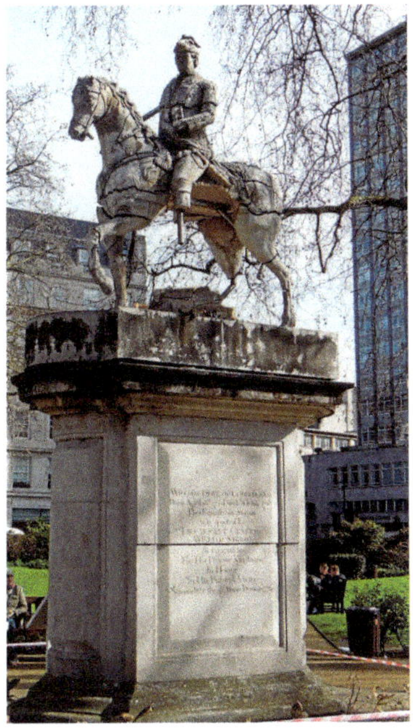

In Cavendish Square Gardens is the long-standing 'empty plinth' with a soap statue of the Duke of Cumberland.

Cavendish Square Gardens is laid out on a circular plan enclosed with a perimeter hedge just north of busy Oxford Street. The plan for the Cavendish Square estate in 1719 heralded the beginnings of Marylebone as a modern urban district of London and set the right tone by attracting the wealthy and fashionable.

John Holles, Duke of Newcastle, bought the Marylebone estate in 1708 and it was then passed to his daughter, Lady Henrietta Cavendish, who married Edward Harley, Second Earl of Oxford and Mortimer. Cavendish Square was to be a spacious square accessed via Holles Street and would include a chapel and a market for the convenience of the inhabitants of the new streets. However, the square never quite rose to the grand heights intended for it.

Distinguished inhabitants who lived around Cavendish Square include the writer Lady Mary Wortley Montagu, Princess Amelia – the third daughter of George II – the painter George Romney, and a plaque at No. 16 Holles Street (now John Lewis) is dedicated to Lord Byron who was born there on the 22 January 1788. Horatio Nelson lived in the square in 1787. Lord Asquith, Liberal Prime Minister (1908–16), lived at No. 20 Cavendish Place between 1895 and 1908. Asquith's opponents gave him the nickname 'Squiffy', a derogatory reference to his fondness for drink.

Quintin Hogg, founder of the Royal Polytechnic, Regent Street, lived at No. 5 between 1885 and 1898. The same address also features in Robert Louis Stevenson's novel *The Strange Case of Dr Jekyll and Mr Hyde* (1886) as the home of Dr Lanyon, Jekyll's former best friend.

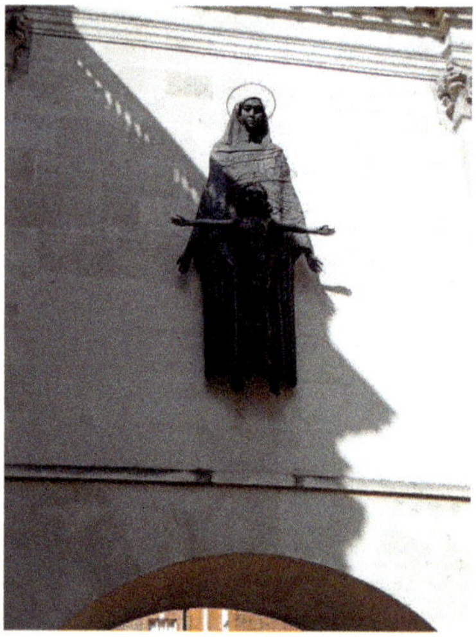

Jacob Epstein's *Virgin and Child* in Cavendish Square.

Much of the Georgian and Regency character of Cavendish Square has been lost as a result of subsequent building during the Victorian and Edwardian eras as well as twentieth-century developments – particularly from the 1970s. The south-west side of the square faces the rear of the flagship John Lewis shop, which began life as a drapery store and opened in 1864.

In 1770, a statue of William, Duke of Cumberland, 'the butcher of Culloden', was placed in the gardens until it was removed in 1868. Only the stone base complete with its inscription remains. The inscription on the plinth is still visible and it reads,

William Duke of Cumberland
Born April 15 1727
Died 31 October 1765

The equestrian statue was erected by Lt-Gen. William Strode. Strode was subsequently court-martialled in 1772 for failing to clothe his troops when on duty in Ireland. However, after an absence of 144 years, a statue of Cumberland on his prancing charger reappeared in July 2012, but this time it was made of soap. The sculpture is the work of Korean artist Meekyoung Shin and was commissioned to go on display for one year.

Also in the gardens is a single statue of Lord George Bentinck, descendant of Lord Harley, dating from 1851 and sculpted by Thomas Campbell.

At the north side of the square are two Grade II-listed 1770 town houses with an unusual Palladian-style ornate bridge between them. In the late nineteenth century, Nos 11, 12 and 13 Cavendish Square were acquired by the Convent of the Holy Child of Jesus. Following bomb damage during the Second World War, the sisters commissioned the architect Louis Osman to restore the houses and create a bridge between the two. Osman asked Jacob Epstein to sculpt a 'Virgin and Child' in lead (used from the bombed roof of No. 12) that would levitate above the arch. Epstein's work was unveiled in 1953.

**Nearest tube:** Oxford Circus.

# 5. Chester Square

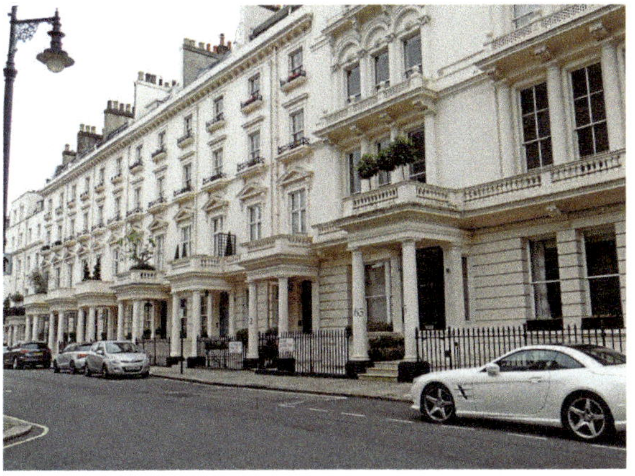

Chester Square houses.

Chester Square is near to Eaton Square and is one of three garden squares built by the Grosvenor family when they developed Belgravia in the nineteenth century. Chester Square, which had the reputation of being Britain's most expensive address, is named after the city of Chester, near Eaton Hall, the ancestral home of the Grosvenor family. The gardens, which are Grade II-listed, are not open to the public. Designed by Thomas Cundy, the Gothic church of St Michael in Chester Square was built, along with the rest of the square, in 1844.

Chester Square lists among its well-known residents Roman Abramovich (main owner of Chelsea Football Club), nineteenth-century writers Matthew Arnold and Mary Shelley (author of *Frankenstein*), actress Julie Andrews, musicians Mick Jagger and Marianne Faithful, violinist Yehudi Menuhin and former Prime Minister Margaret Thatcher.

**Nearest tube:** Victoria.

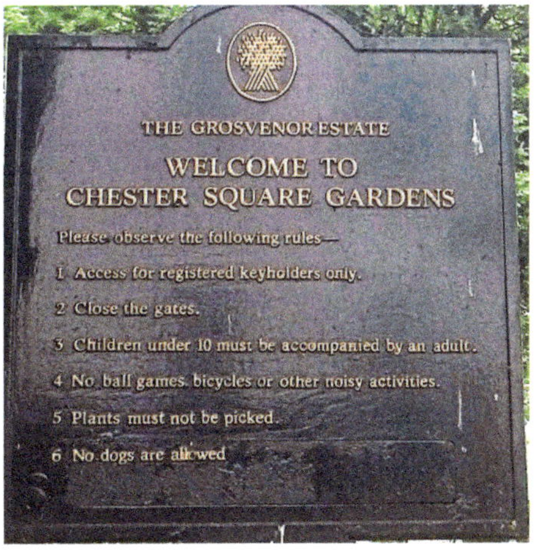


The notice in Chester Square for use of the gardens.

# 6. Drury Lane Gardens

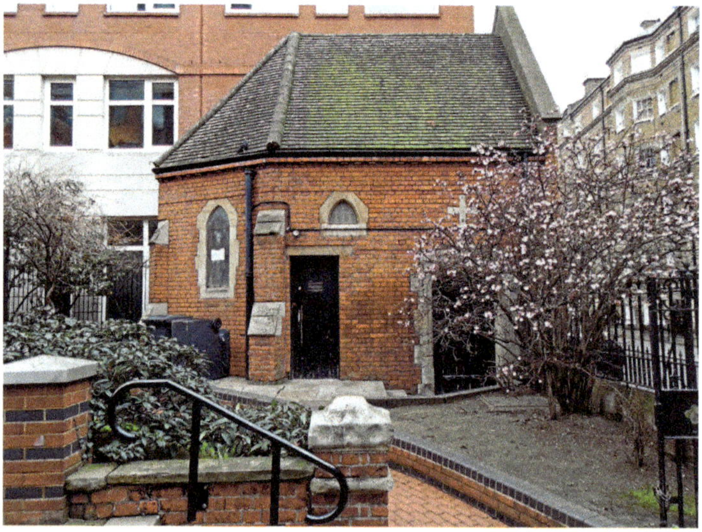

The mortuary in Drury Lane Gardens.

Drury Lane Gardens, created in 1877, was a former burial ground of St Martin-in-the-Fields. We have Mrs Isabella 'Bella' Basil Holmes to thank for much of the information regarding London graveyards and burial grounds that would have been otherwise lost. She married Basil Holmes, who was secretary to the Metropolitan Public Gardens, which was founded in 1882. In her book *The London Burial Grounds* (1896), she described Drury Lane Gardens as 'so disgustingly overcrowded that no burials could take place there without the disturbance of other bodies, which were crowded into pits dug in the ground, and covered with boards'.

Drury Lane Gardens (which can be found off Russell Street alongside the Crown Court Church of Scotland) was the first burial ground to be made into a public garden in Westminster following its closure as a result of the Burial Acts of 1852. The gardens, which are small but attractive, contain a number of tombstones that lie along the north boundary wall. The red-brick Gothic mortuary and lodge survive either side of the entrance, together with gate piers of 1880. A playground, sports court and hard landscaping mainly occupy the raised garden. There are also benches shaded by a pergola with shrubberies, bedding displays and a drinking fountain.

The gardens feature in *Bleak House* (1853) by Charles Dickens where Esther's father, Captain Hawdon, was buried and where Lady Dedlock died on the steps by the entrance. Dickens described the place as 'a hemmed-in churchyard, pestiferous and obscene, whence malignant diseases are communicated to the bodies of our dear brothers and sisters who have not departed'.

**Nearest tube:** Covent Garden.

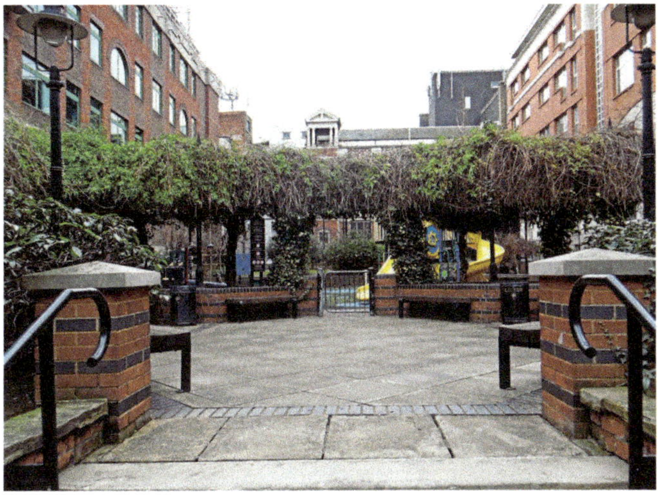

The entrance to Drury Lane Gardens.

## 7. Eaton Square

Eaton Square is in Belgravia and is one of London's most prestigious addresses. The square is oblong in shape and arranged around six private gardens. It is named after Eaton Hall, the Grosvenor country house in Cheshire. When George III acquired Buckingham Palace in 1761, nearby Belgravia and Mayfair became excellent bases from which to court the king. In 1824, the 2nd Marquis of Westminster, Richard Grosvenor, who owned most of the land that is now Belgravia, Pimlico and Mayfair, commissioned master builder Thomas Cubitt to develop the square into large, terraced houses with the first section of the square laid out in 1827.

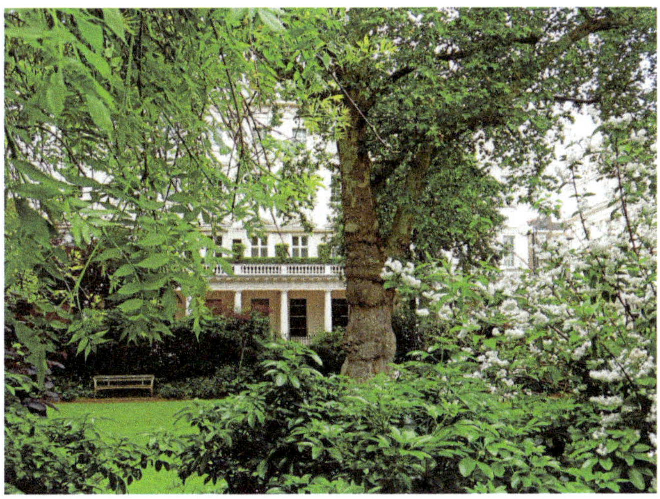

Looking across Eaton Square Gardens.

The large, mainly white, stucco terraced houses are built in a classical style with four or five main storeys as well as an attic, basement and mews house at the rear. St Peter's Church, built between 1824 and 1827, is at the east end of the square.

Past and present residents include former Prime Ministers Stanley Baldwin and Neville Chamberlain, actors Vivien Leigh, Roger Moore, Sean Connery and Rex Harrison, food writer Nigella Lawson and Sarah, Duchess of York. No. 100 Eaton Square is home to the Duke of Westminster.

Super-wealthy foreigners own many properties in the square. However, this is not a new phenomenon. In his 1904 novel *The Golden Bowl*, Henry James made Eaton Square the residence of Adam Verver, a very wealthy American who has made his millions through skyscrapers and elevators.

Other literary works that feature the exclusiveness of Eaton Square include, *Wise Children* (1991) by Angela Carter and *The Bertrams* (1859) by Anthony Trollope. It is also the address of fictional radio detective Paul Temple who lived at No. 26A. In the television series *Downtown Abbey*, the character of Lady Rosamund Painswick maintained an address in Eaton Square while the Bellamy family of *Upstairs, Downstairs* lived at Eaton Place.

At nearby Eaton Mews, a painted ghost sign, which was restored in 2011, reads, 'Horse Infirmary and shoeing forge'. The stables began life in 1823 and since 1850 it provided commercial services such as a veterinary, wheelwright and carriage repair shop and eventually a car garage.

**Nearest tube:** Victoria.

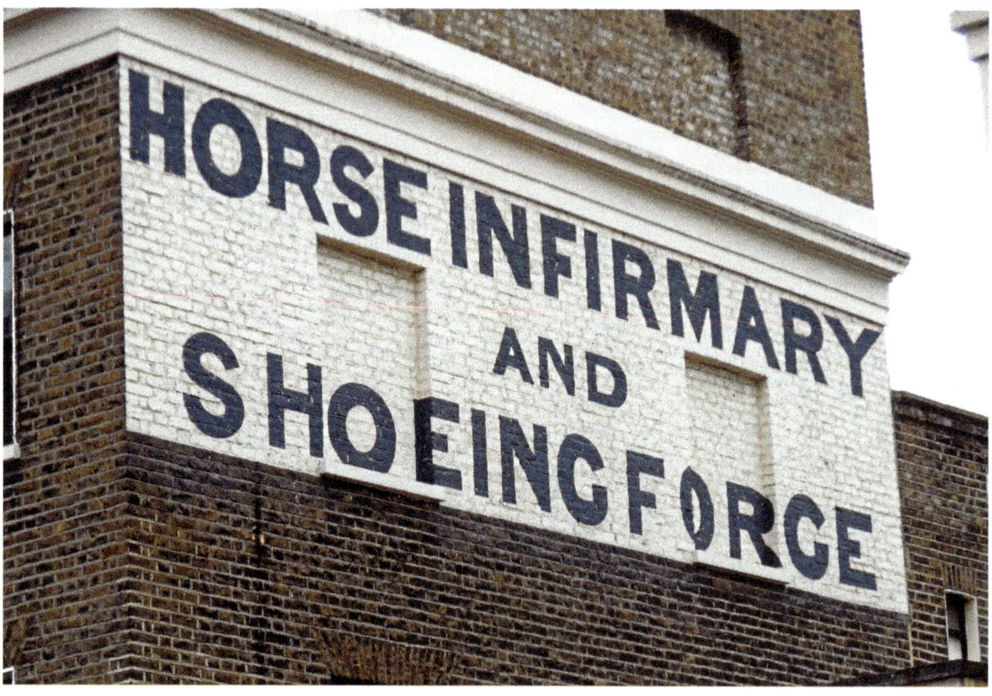


A restored ghost sign at nearby Eaton Mews.

# 8. Golden Square

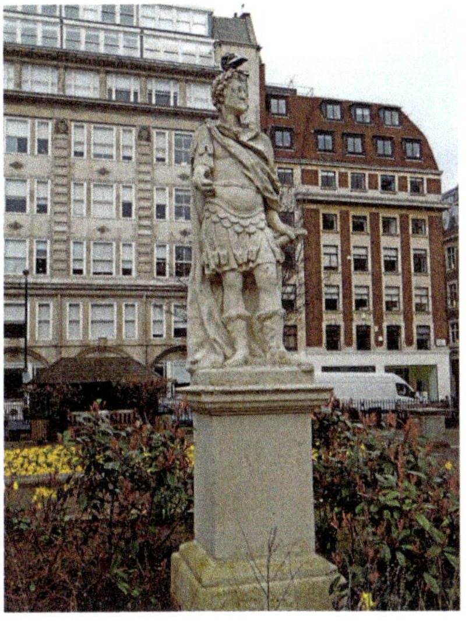

The statue of George II erected in 1753 in Golden Square Gardens.

Golden Square lies in Soho, a short distance to the east of Regent Street. The development of Golden Square began around 1670 on what initially was a very prestigious project containing many embassies and residences of the political elite. The curious name 'Golden' possibly derives from 'gelding', the land having been used previously as pasture for horses.

By the nineteenth century, the square became less favoured as those residents affluent enough to do so took themselves off to the exclusive new developments taking place further west in Belgravia or Mayfair. Soho then developed a somewhat raffish reputation. Many of the residences around the square became multiple occupancies. Charles Dickens alluded to this with these words:

> Its boarding-houses are musical, and the notes of pianos and harps float in the evening time round the head of the mournful statue ... in the centre of the Square. On a summer's night, windows are thrown open, and groups of swarthy moustached men are seen by the passer-by, lounging at the casement, and smoking fearfully. Sounds of gruff voices practising vocal music invade the evening's silence, and the fumes of choice tobacco scent the air.
>
> *The Life and Adventures of Nicholas Nickleby* (1838)

William Pitt the Elder, who led the government of Great Britain twice in the middle of the eighteenth century, was born in the square in 1708. Nos 32 and 33 are on the site of the first specialist throat hospital in Britain, then known as the Hospital for Diseases of the Throat. This lasted as a hospital until 1985. There is a Westminster City Council plaque to Sir Morrell Mackenzie (1837–92), one of its early leading figures. Unfortunately, Mackenzie blotted his copybook in 1887 when he examined Crown Prince Frederick of Prussia. It was thought that he had cancer but Mackenzie disagreed. Soon after, cancer was confirmed and some accused Mackenzie of professional neglect.

There is a well-known statue in the gardens erected in 1753. It portrays George II who reigned from 1727 to 1760. However, there is some confusion as to whether the statue is that of George II or Charles II. It was rumoured that the statue was accidentally won at auction when the bidder raised his hand to welcome a friend. The amount of money he paid was so low he decided to give the statue as a gift to the people of Golden Square.

George II had married in 1705 (his wife Caroline died in 1737) and there was never any doubt as to who ruled the roost during their marriage. A popular contemporary ditty went as follows:

> You may strut, dapper George, but 'twill be in vain,
> We know 'tis Queen Caroline, not you, that reign.

An eccentric resident of Golden Square was Vladimir de Pachmann, a virtuoso player of the works of Chopin. He died in 1933 but had spent the previous year taking daily exercise around the boundaries of the square. Pachmann amassed a fabulous collection of jewels worth a fortune. He recklessly carried them loose in his pockets and in his final illness they 'disappeared'. When he died he had virtually no personal possessions.

Beneath Golden Square lies a communal burial pit containing untold numbers of the bodies of victims of the 1665 Great Plague, one of the many visitations of the bubonic plague to the metropolis. During the Second World War, the enclosing iron railings were removed for salvage and an air-raid shelter was dug beneath the garden.

Many of the buildings around the square are occupied by businesses engaged in media and communications. The gardens are open to the public and much frequented by office workers.

**Nearest tube:** Oxford Street, Tottenham Court Road, Leicester Square, Piccadilly Circus.

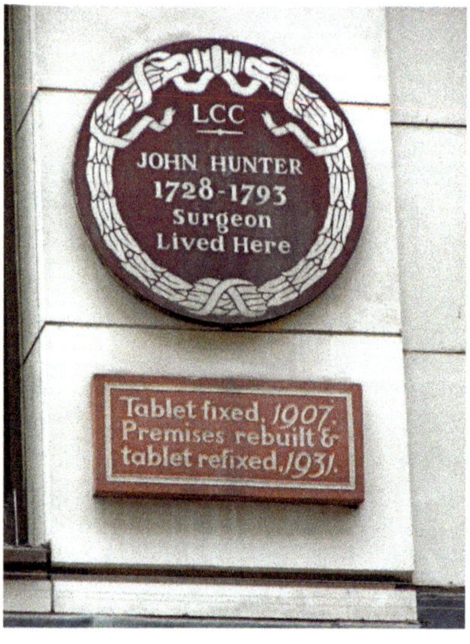


The plaque to the famous eighteenth-century surgeon John Hunter in Golden Square, Soho.

# 9. Grosvenor Square

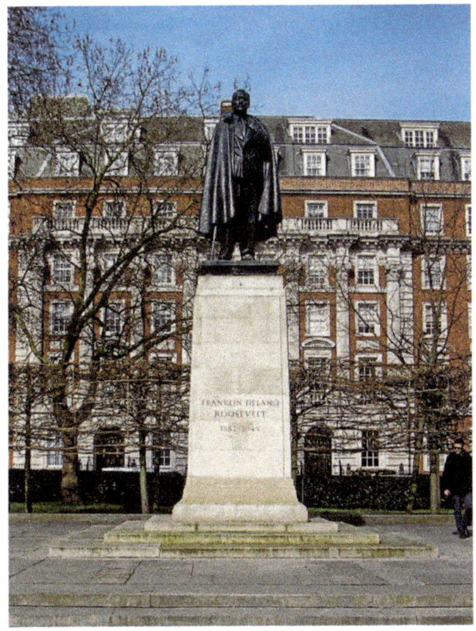

The large statue of Franklin D. Roosevelt in Grosvenor Square Gardens.

This large Mayfair square is a short walk south of Bond Street Tube Station. Building of the square commenced in 1723 and was completed in 1731. It was always intended to be a prestigious residential development catering for London's most affluent social elite. Unlike many other developments, it has retained a social exclusivity due to careful monitoring and management by the Grosvenor estate, of which it effectively forms the focal point. Its favoured position close to Hyde Park helps to explain its continuing desirability. Only two of the square's original buildings survive although they are much altered – Nos 9 and 38.

Grosvenor Square has been the traditional home of the official American presence in London since John Adams, the second president of the United States, established the first american mission in 1785 to the Court of St James's. This is the royal court for the sovereign of the United Kingdom and where all ambassadors and high commissioners are formally received. Adams lived at No. 9 from 1785 to 1788 in the house that still stands on the corner of Brook Street and Duke Street.

The Canadian government purchased the former American Embassy of 1938–60, but in 1960 a new United States Embassy was built on the western side of Grosvenor Square. In 2008, the United States government chose a site for a new embassy in the Nine Elms area of Wandsworth. The old embassy is to be converted into a luxury hotel as part of a £1 billion restoration of Grosvenor Square. However, because of the listed status of the Grosvenor building, new owners will not be allowed to change the façade, which includes the 35-foot wingspread eagle above the main entrance.

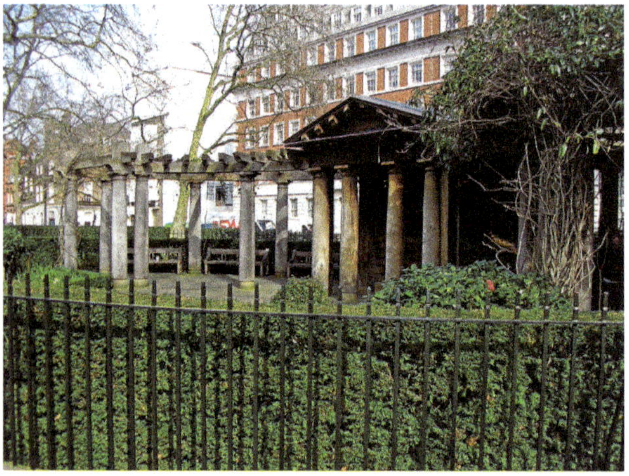

The 9/11 Remembrance Garden, Grosvenor Square Gardens.

The square gained the nickname 'Eisenhower Plaza' during the Second World War because so many of its buildings were occupied by the American military. There is a statue of President F. D. Roosevelt (1882–1945) who was seen as being largely responsible for creating the political climate that brought the US into the Second World War. This decision was immediately precipitated by the Japanese attack on Pearl Harbour. In the 1920s, Roosevelt contracted polio, afterwards only standing with difficulty and having to use a walking stick. There were proposals for the statue to portray him seated but his widow, Eleanor, insisted on a standing figure. It is bronze, 10 feet high and was unveiled in 1946. A plaque at No. 20 indicates the location of Eisenhower's headquarters in 1942. There is also a statue of former actor and president Ronald Reagan.

The Americans retain a very strong presence in Grosvenor Square Gardens. A memorial to the Second World War Eagle Squadrons can be seen – in the form of an obelisk topped by a bronze eagle. Another memorial remembers the sixty-seven British victims of the attack on the World Trade Centre in 2001. It is surrounded by an oak pergola and pavilion which bears the words of Elizabeth II, 'Grief is the price we pay for love'.

In March and October 1968, Grosvenor Square was the scene of large and ill-tempered demonstrations against US involvement in Vietnam outside the American Embassy. The gardens in the centre of the square are managed by the Royal Parks and are open to the public. Grosvenor Square is second only to Lincoln's Inn Fields in terms of size.

The former No. 40, now part of a hotel, was, in the late eighteenth century, the residence of the Countess of Strathmore, a young and extremely wealthy widow. Unfortunately, the advances of Capt. Andrew Stoney, a charming and plausible rogue, succeeded and he systematically worked his way through his wife's fortune, abused her physically and ostentatiously took a mistress. The countess eventually obtained a divorce and Stoney died in prison in 1810.

George I (1660–1727) was not an impressive monarch. Lord Chesterfield described him as 'an honest, dull German gentleman' and stated he was 'lazy and inactive'. A proposal to erect a statue to George I in St James's Square failed due to a lack of subscribers and it was left to Sir Richard Grosvenor in 1726 to erect an equestrian statue of gilded lead in the square at a cost of 250 guineas. In 1727, a Jacobite mob pulled off one of the horse's legs and a rather lewd verse was attached to the King's neck. The statue was known still to be in situ as late as 1838 but it subsequently disappeared and its fate remains unknown. No fewer than eleven royal mistresses have occupied dwellings in Grosvenor Square although, perhaps fortunately, not all at the same time.

Grosvenor Square appears in a number of well-known novels and plays including *Little Dorrit* (1857) by Charles Dickens and *The Importance of Being Earnest* (1895), *Lady Windermere's Fan* (1893) and *An Ideal Husband* (1895) by Oscar Wilde.

**Nearest tube:** Marble Arch, Bond Street.

## 10. Hanover Square

Hanover Square is located in Mayfair off Oxford Street and is south along Harewood Place. The square was named in honour of George I, the Elector of Hanover. The 1701 Act of Settlement excluded Roman Catholics from succeeding to the throne and, in 1714, George I from Hanover became the first Hanoverian monarch, hence the naming of the square.

The square was laid out from 1713 and soon developed as a fashionable residential address. Soon afterwards, St George's Church, designed by John James between 1721 and 1724, was built to the south (on St George Street) as one of London's planned 'fifty new churches' – although only around a dozen were built. St George's established a reputation for being the capital's most fashionable venue for society weddings.

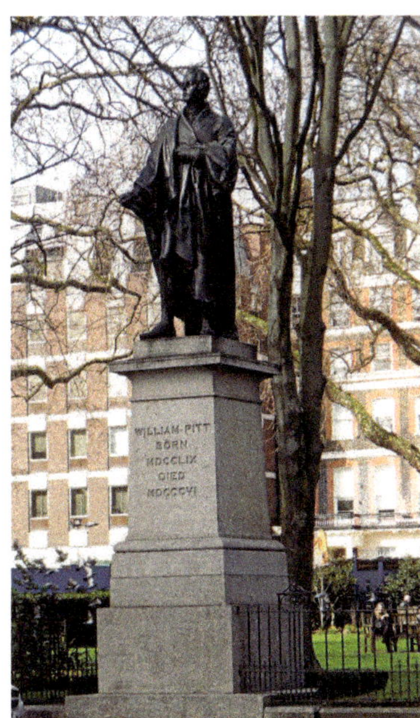


The statue of William Pitt, Hanover Square Gardens.

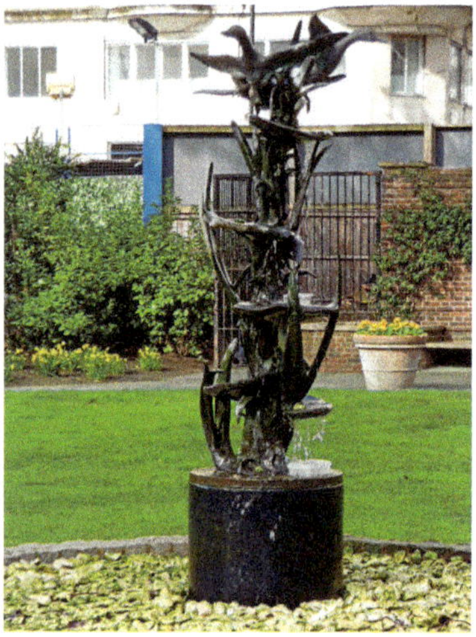

Hanover Square Gardens' sculpture.

While a few of the eighteenth-century houses remain largely intact, most of the square has been reconstructed on a number of occasions. It is now almost entirely occupied by offices. The gardens have several old and new statues and sculptures. On the south side is a statue of William Pitt the Younger (1759–1806) by Sir Francis Legatt Chantrey, which stands on a lofty granite plinth. It was erected in 1831 and survived an attempt by Reform Bill agitators to pull it down on the day it was opened.

After the Second World War, the garden was re-landscaped with a small ornamental pond, a fountain near the north end and a bronze sculpture in the centre of the pond. The gardens were originally provided for the private use of inhabitants of surrounding houses. A small picturesque building is located just outside the north side of the garden enclosure. On the north side of the central gardens is a cabman's shelter where a good breakfast can be had. See the section on Russell Square for further details about these shelters. As with some other gardens, a table tennis facility has been installed and has proved to be popular.

**Nearest tube:** Oxford Circus.

# 11. Leicester Square

Leicester Square is synonymous with the bustle of the West End and its theatres and shops. The square, originally a gentrified residential area, changed when retail developments took place and theatres were established in the nineteenth century. The square was refurbished in 2012 for the London Olympic Games and also reopened in time for the Queen's Diamond Jubilee.

In 1630, Lord Leicester built Leicester House (demolished in the 1790s) but was required to develop public walks on the remaining part of the common land initially called Leicester

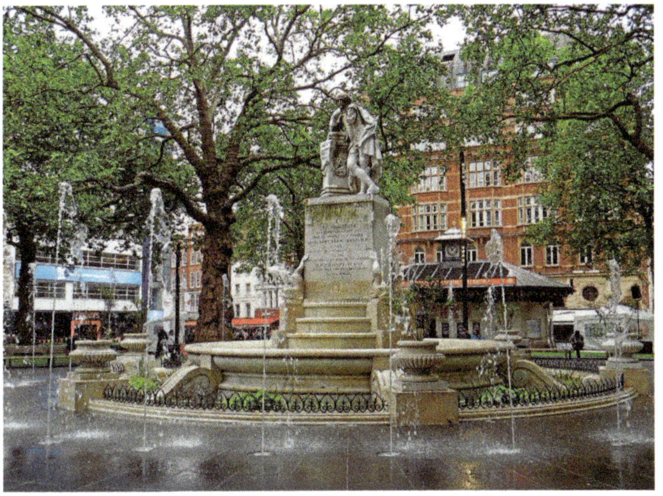

The statue of William Shakespeare with fountain at Leicester Square.

Fields. This included the small park that was originally available for common use on Lammas Day (12 August) for activities such as clothes washing and cattle herding. A statue of George I stood in the centre from 1748, but was removed following vandalism in 1871.

In 1874, Albert Grant MP purchased and presented the newly laid out garden with a Shakespeare memorial fountain (created by Giovanni Fontana) in the centre. In the twentieth century, Leicester Square was progressively rebuilt, becoming the centre of the entertainment industry. The gardens inevitably suffered heavy use and were re-landscaped in 1993 when the statues and fountain were restored and a prominent theatre ticket booth was erected.

At each corner of the fountain are busts of former residents: artist William Hogarth who lived at No. 30 between 1733 and 1764; surgeon John Hunter; scientist Sir Isaac Newton; and painter and President of the Royal Academy, Sir Joshua Reynolds who lived at No. 47 from 1760 until his death in 1792. No. 47 is now Fanum House.

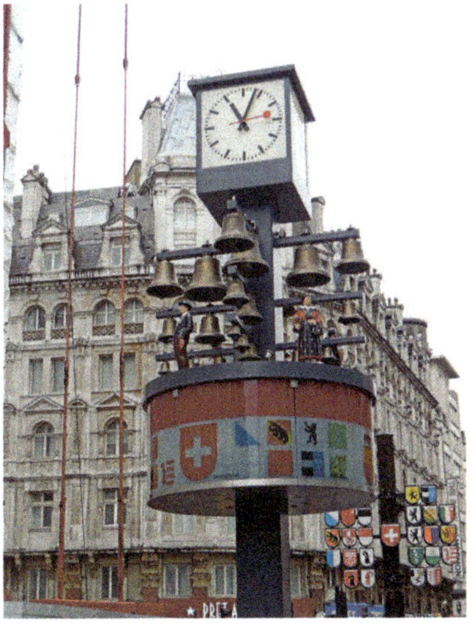

The Leicester Square glockenspiel.

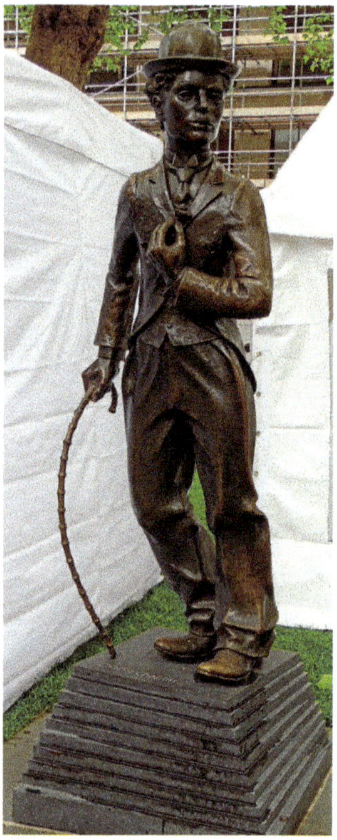

Leicester Square's statue of Charlie Chaplin.

The famous Alhambra Theatre, built in 1854, once stood on the east side of the square. It was demolished in 1936 and replaced by the Odeon Cinema. The Empire of Varieties opened in 1881 but soon gained a notorious reputation for high-class prostitutes who frequented the theatre. It eventually closed in 1927 and was replaced by the Empire Cinema.

The square was pedestrianised in the 1980s and a fibreglass statue of Charlie Chaplin was unveiled in 1981. In 1993, an electricity-generating plant was built beneath the northern portion of the square. Antony Clayton, in his book *Subterranean City: Beneath the Streets of London* (2000), states that the electricity sub-station beneath Leicester Square is entered by a disguised trap door to the left of the half-price ticket booth, a structure that also doubles as a ventilation shaft.

An unusual sight is the Swiss glockenspiel, a gift from Switzerland and Liechtenstein. The glockenspiel is a 10-metre-tall steel structure that has a carillon with twenty-seven bells. Below the bells are eleven wooden figures of animals and people in historical dress. On the hour during the afternoon, the figures walk in a procession accompanied by the chiming of carillon bells. The whole structure is crowned with a Swiss clock.

Leicester Square Tube Station is reputed to be the most popular route for tourists as well as the shortest distance between tube stations – Leicester Square to Covent Garden on the Piccadilly line is only 0.16 miles.

**Nearest tube:** Leicester Square.

# 12. Lower and Upper Grosvenor Gardens

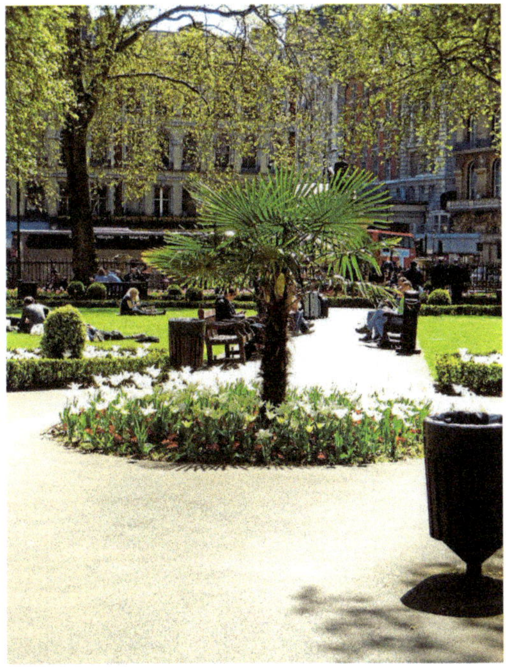

Lower Grosvenor Gardens: a peaceful oasis in a very busy area.

Lower Grosvenor Gardens is a triangular London square a short distance from Victoria Station. Amid the noise and rush of traffic between Victoria Station and nearby Buckingham Palace sits this patch of green that is generally filled with office workers eating lunch as well as people just resting or visiting.

Named after the Grosvenor family, both Lower Grosvenor Gardens and nearby Upper Grosvenor Gardens date from 1864 and were designed to complement the French Renaissance-style houses which overlook the two squares.

Lower Grosvenor Gardens was redesigned in 1952 and dedicated to Marshall Foch, a decorated hero of the First World War. The gardens, which are surrounded by a variety of listed buildings, contain flowers with bedding displays, an equestrian statue of Marshall Foch, which stands at the entrance, and two unusual lodges studded with seashells. The lodges were designed for the use of the park's gardeners.

Upper Grosvenor Gardens, another triangular square, is almost adjacent to Lower Grosvenor Gardens and was opened to the public in 1980. Prior to that, they were only for the use of nearby residents. Notable features include an impressive bronze sculpture named *Lioness Chasing a Lesser Kudu* by Jonathan Kenworthy and a monument to the Rifle Brigade (1924–25) by John Tweed that stands on the north-eastern corner.

**Nearest tube:** Victoria.

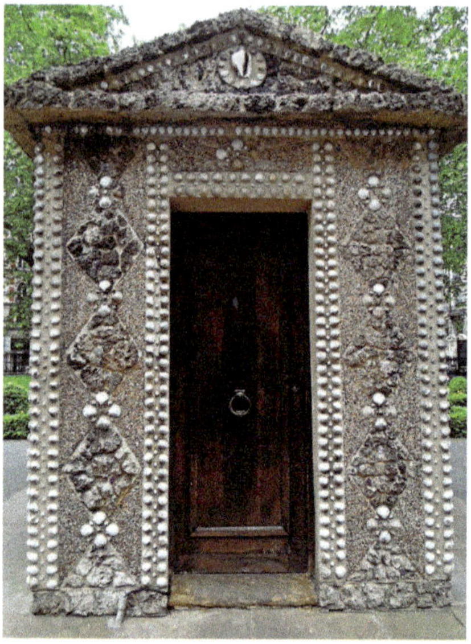

The 'Seashell Lodge' in Lower Grosvenor Gardens.

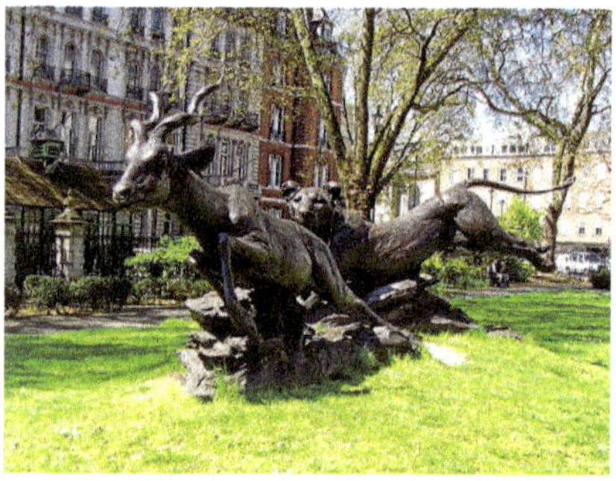

*Lioness Chasing a Lesser Kudu* by Jonathan Kenworthy in Upper Grosvenor Gardens.

# 13. Manchester Square

Manchester Square Gardens, in keeping with a number of gardens in Marylebone, is private. It is a short distance north of Oxford Street along Duke Street and is one of the smaller, but better, preserved Georgian squares in Central London. It is named after the Duke of Manchester and was built between 1776 and 1788 on land belonging to the Portman estate. The garden layout today is little changed from its late eighteenth-century layout. A mansion once known as Manchester House, and later as Hertford House, dominates the northern side of Manchester Square. This is now the home of the Wallace Collection, a major collection of fine and decorative arts, as well as a magnificent armoury collected in the eighteenth and nineteenth centuries by the first four Marquises of Hertford and Sir Richard Wallace. In the forecourt of Hertford House is a cast-iron drinking fountain designed by Charles Lebourg in 1878.

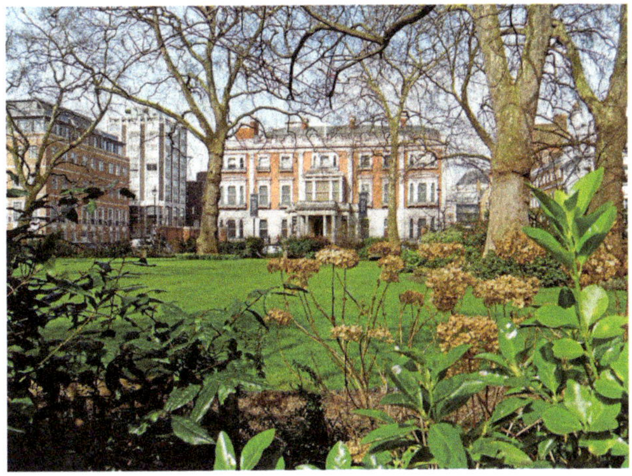

Manchester Square Gardens with Hertford House, home to the Wallace Collection, in the background.

A note of interest regarding the road that runs to the north of Hertford House, George Street, is that No. 34 claims to have been the site of the first Asian restaurant in London, opened in 1810 by Sake Dean Mahomed to cater for London's many Anglo-Indians.

Famous residents of the square have included John Hughlings Jackson, the English neurologist who lived at No. 3, Julius Benedict, the German-born composer who lived at No. 2 and Alfred Lord Milner, the British statesman and colonial administrator who lived at No. 14. The hostess, Lady Blessington, lived there briefly before she married Charles John Gardiner, 1st Earl of Blessington in 1818. The composer Sir Julius Benedict (1804–85) lived and died at No. 2 Manchester Square. Just south of the square along Duke Street is a blue plaque to the liberator of Latin America, Simon Bolivar (1783–1830) who lodged in these premises in 1810.

To the north of the square is Manchester Street where, in 1814, the self-described religious prophetess, Joanna Southcott died. In 1792, she received divine revelations, which saw her amass a following of some 20,000 people by 1815. Southcott left a locked box with instructions that it be opened only in the presence of all the bishops at a time of national crisis. In 1928, the alleged box was opened but, disappointingly, revealed nothing of interest.

During the Second World War, trenches were dug in the garden of the square and tanks for emergency water were erected. A small bomb and incendiary devices fell in the garden.

**Nearest tube:** Bond Street.

## 14. Montagu Square

Montagu Square is one of a number of squares in Marylebone and lies north of Marble Arch Tube Station. The brick houses of Montagu Square were built from 1810 by David Porter and named after Mrs Elizabeth Montagu who lived nearby in Portman Square.

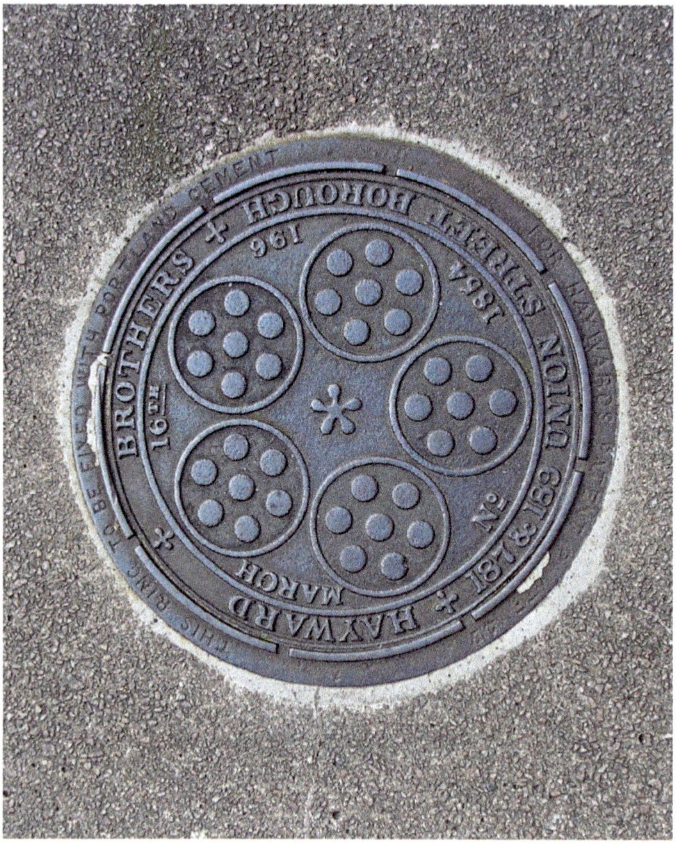


Montagu Square. One of the many coal-hole covers set in the pavements in this part of London. Some people take rubbings of them.

Montagu Square is a purely residential square in Westminster. The long, narrow gardens in the centre of the square are private.

Ringo Starr, of Beatles fame, leased Flat 1, No. 34, in 1965, shortly before he married. He and his wife lived there briefly before moving to Surrey. He retained the lease of the flat, which was rented by fellow Beatle Paul McCartney who converted part of it into a basic recording studio. He moved on and the flat was let in late 1966 to the American rock guitarist Jimmy Hendrix and Gordon Haskell who was the bass player of the band The Fleur de Lys. Though hugely talented, Hendrix was a volatile character who, on one occasion, threw whitewash all over the walls. He proved to be a nightmare tenant and Starr had to evict him.

Another Beatle, John Lennon, was also associated with the flat in the square. Lennon was attracting a great deal of attention on account of his relationship with Yoko Ono. Lennon became estranged from his wife and moved into the flat with Yoko in June 1968. There were vague and unfulfilled plans to turn the flat into a museum of rock music. On 23 October 2010, Yoko unveiled a blue plaque, which states that 'John Lennon, 1940–1980, musician and songwriter, lived here in 1968.'

Anthony Trollope, the prolific author of around fifty novels, lived at No. 39 from 1873 to 1880. He was generally regarded as a disagreeable and overbearing man who enjoyed being objectionable. On one occasion, he repeatedly interrupted the speaker in a meeting by shouting, 'I disagree with everything you say.' Having reduced the poor man to silence, he then added, 'What was it you said?' Trollope is credited as the inventor of the pillar box, probably in 1854. He was the clerk to the surveyor of the South Western district of the Post Office. He invented the idea of the box rather than actually designing it. The first pillar box was opened at St Helier in the Channel Islands.

Just after 5.15 p.m. on 8 December 2014, a property tycoon who had made and then, apparently, lost millions of pounds, fell from the penthouse at No. 33 and was impaled on the railings.

Directly south of Montagu Square is Montague Street. In July 1822, the Bishop of Clogher, Percy Jocelyn, was misguided enough to enter a pub in what is now Lower Regent Street wearing his full episcopal apparel. He succumbed to the allure of a private of the 1st Regiment of Guards and the couple withdrew to a back room where they were seen by several witnesses engaged in an act described as 'gross indecency' and both were arrested. The latter was imprisoned but the Bishop escaped abroad where he died in 1845.

**Nearest tube:** Baker Street, Marble Arch.

# 15. Mount Street Gardens

This delightful secluded garden in the heart of Mayfair is hidden behind houses, a large red-brick mansion block and has two churches at each end. The gardens provide an oasis of calm and beauty and a visit will be well rewarded.

The site was established in 1723 as a burial ground (closed in 1854) for the parish church of St George Hanover Square. Some of the gravestones have been removed to the gardens' tool shed at the western part of the gardens. As the population increased, and the area expanded from 1725, a parish workhouse (relocated to a larger site in 1871) was located there as well as a watchmen's quarters and watch-house to the north of the site. By the late nineteenth century, redevelopments provided the current spacious character of the gardens one finds today. Mount Street was named after Mount Field, the remains of fortifications erected during the English Civil War.

The gardens contain many large London plane trees and the benches have been donated by or in memory of people (including many Americans) who have used and loved the space throughout the years, such as Joe Bleich (1910–90), 'An American who could not find a park like this in New York City.'

The temperature in the gardens is said to be several degrees above the surrounding area, thus facilitating other trees such as an Australian mimosa, three dawn redwoods and a Canary Island date palm. They also add to the fragrant aroma as you enter the gardens. Not surprisingly, the gardens are designated as a Site of Importance for Nature Conservation. An information board offers a guide to the many species of bird that frequent the gardens. There are also two red K2 London phone kiosks outside the entrance.

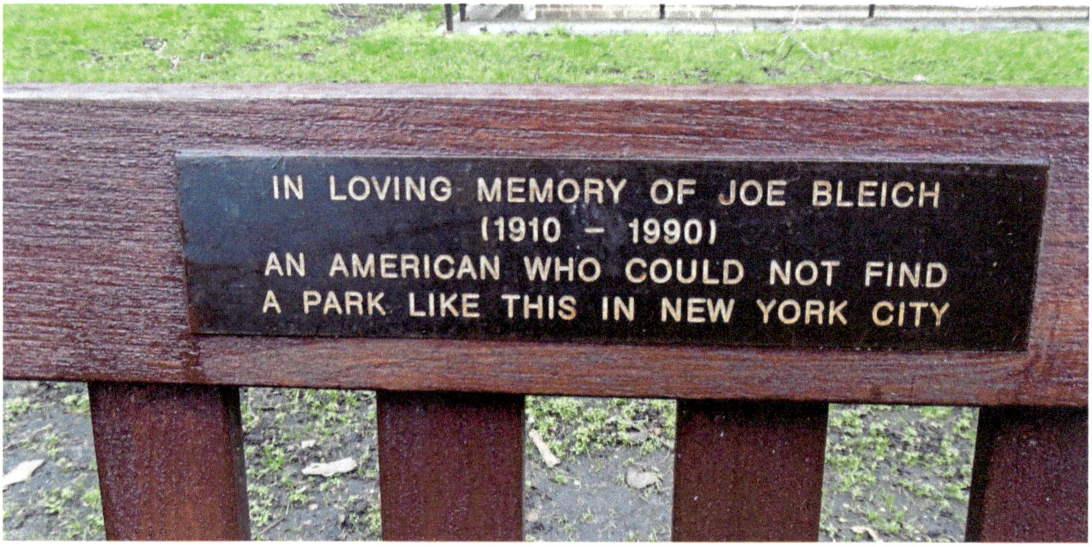


Mount Street Gardens. An American in London.

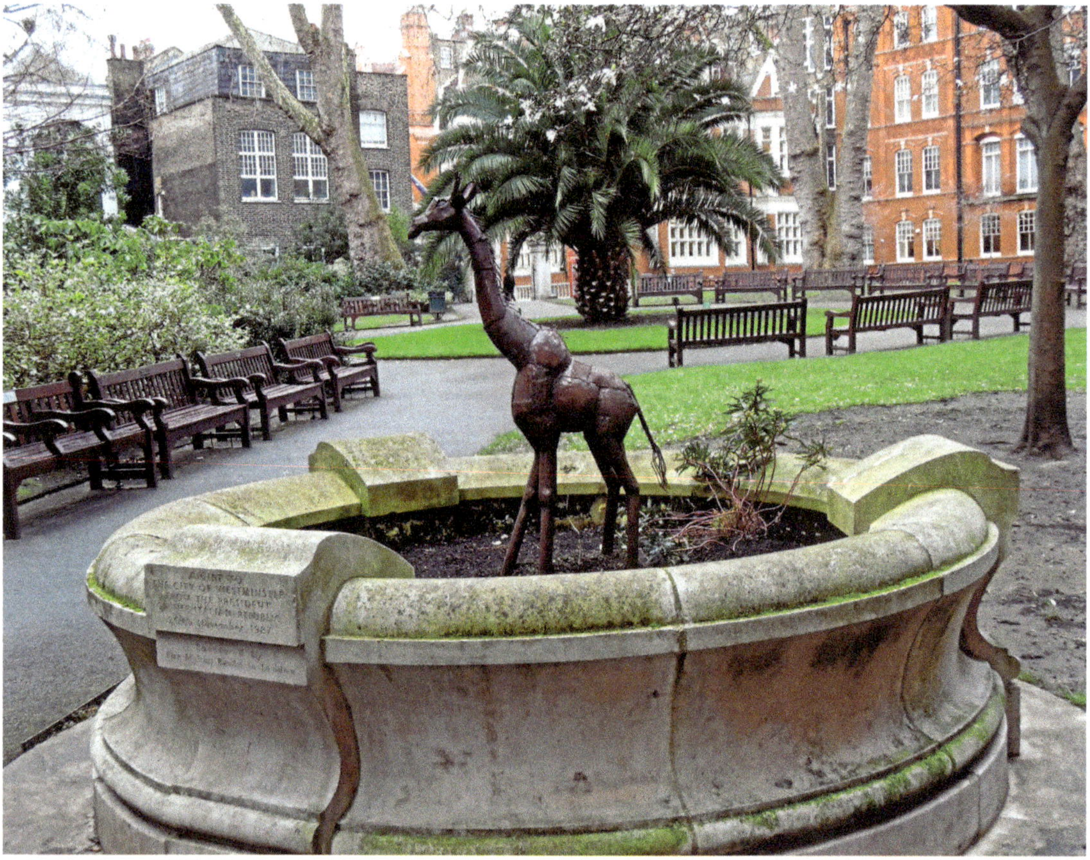

'Giraffe' in Mount Street Gardens.

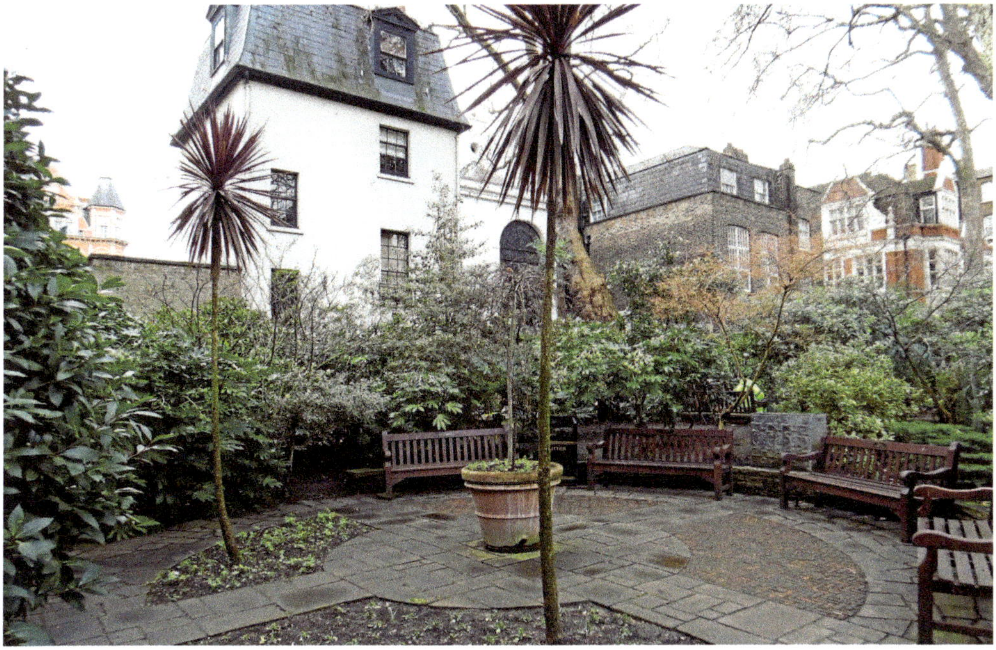

Tranquillity in Mount Street Gardens.

Features to look for include a birdbath and a bronze drinking fountain depicting a rearing horse, designed by Sir Ernest George and Harold Peto. There are also two ornamental lead cisterns inscribed 'T.F. 1725' in the gardens. There is a sculpture of a giraffe with the dedication, 'A gift to the City of Westminster from the president of the Italian Republic 20th November 1987'. In addition, there is a temporary 2016 sculpture of a horse's head called *Fire* by Nic Fiddian-Green.

At the east end is the Roman Catholic Church of the Immaculate Conception – familiarly known as Farm Street Church – run by the Society of Jesus in Mayfair. The church is a Grade II-listed building built between 1844 and 1849. It is decorated in a neo-Gothic style with a high altar by Augustus Pugin (1812–52), an English architect, designer, artist and critic remembered for his interior design of the Palace of Westminster. In his book *England's Thousand Best Churches* (1999), Simon Jenkins describes the Farm Street Church as 'Gothic Revival at its most sumptuous'.

Grosvenor Chapel is on the west side and has been the spiritual home to a number of famous people, such as the radical John Wilkes (1725–97); there is a plaque to Wilkes in the chapel's upstairs gallery. Others include Florence Nightingale and US President Dwight D. Eisenhower. The chapel features in the wedding scene at the start of the Richard Curtis film *Love Actually* (2003).

No. 105 Mount Street, to the north of the gardens, served as Winston Churchill's first bachelor flat between 1900 and 1905. Just outside the west entrance is a Mayfair Public Library, which dates from 1894.

**Nearest tube:** Bond Street, Green Park.

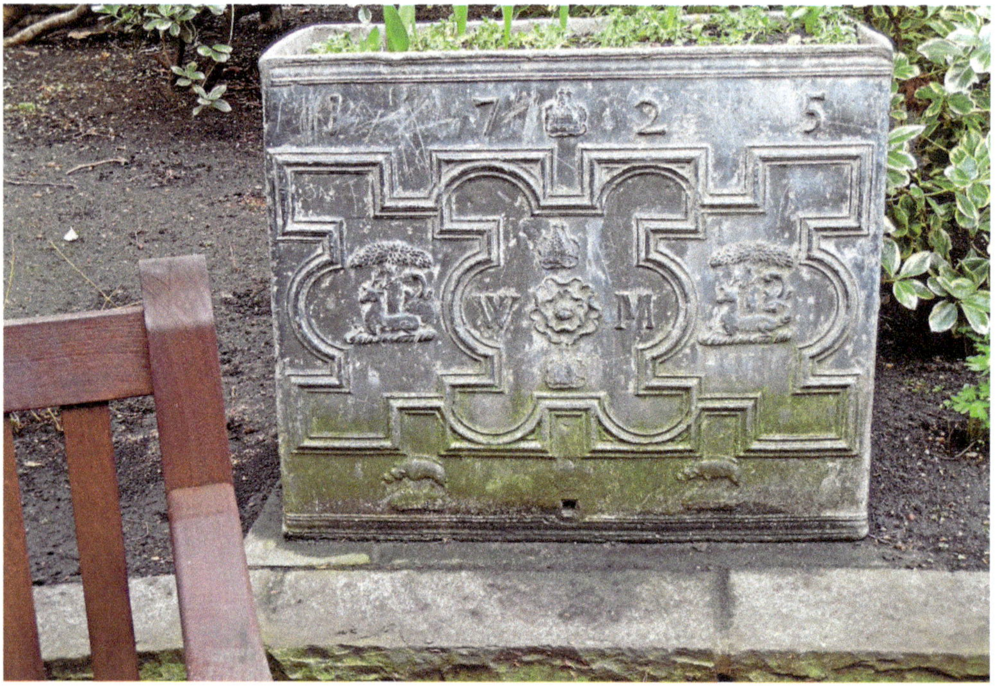


Mount Street Gardens cistern, 1725.

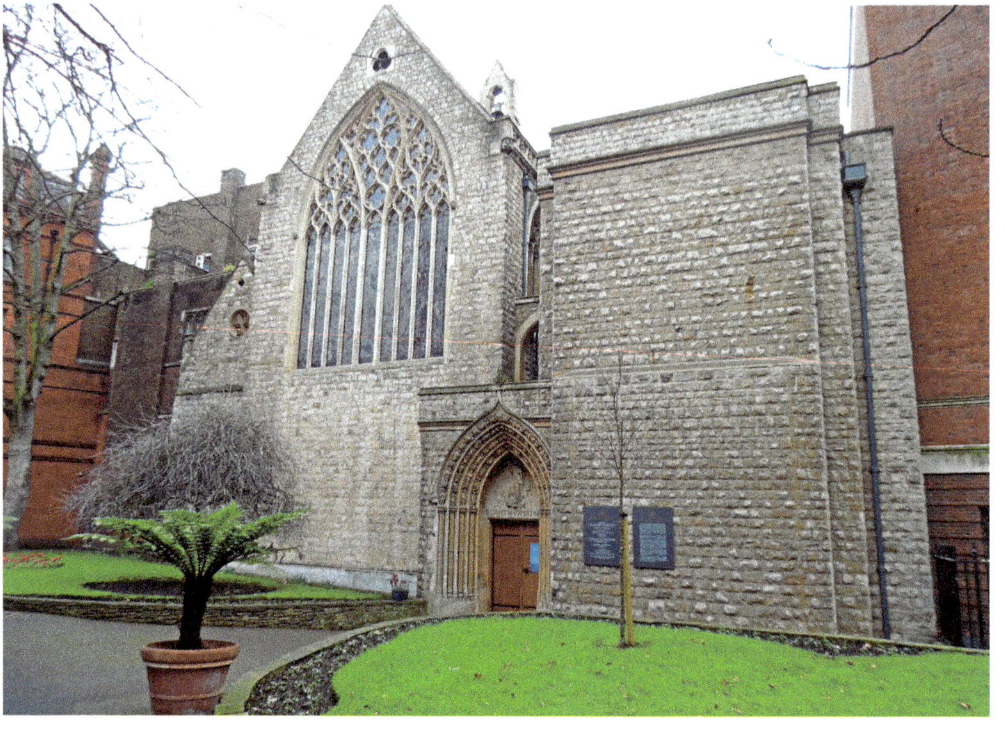

Mount Street Gardens and the Church of the Immaculate Conception.

# 16. Parliament Square

Parliament Square is located opposite the Houses of Parliament and can be best reached from Westminster Tube Station. Sir Charles Barry laid out the square in 1868. It was designed to open up an approach to the rebuilt Houses of Parliament, of which he was the architect. It was also intended to ease the flow of traffic in the locality, already proving to be something of a problem.

Despite this, there is much to see in and around Parliament Square including Westminster Abbey, the Cenotaph, the Cabinet War Rooms, St James's Park and the vista across the nearby River Thames. Various official buildings including the Houses of Parliament, Whitehall, Downing Street and the Supreme Court are within close reach of the square.

Being so close to parliament, the square contains a large amount of statuary and several are eminent parliamentarians – they include Lord Palmerston who was Prime Minister from 1855–58 and 1859–65. This statue was unveiled in 1876 and has been described as

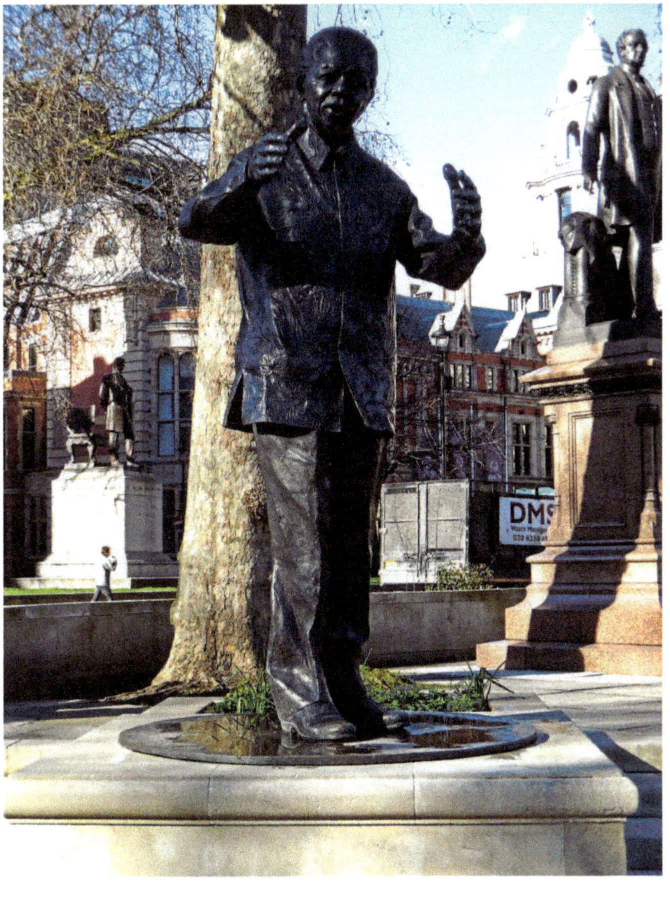

The statue of Nelson Mandela in Parliament Square.

'the best dressed statue in London'. Close by stands the figure of Benjamin Disraeli who was Prime Minister from 1867–68 and 1874–80. A crucial figure in the history of the Conservative Party, he was a heavy smoker and inordinately fond of brandy. To maintain his stamina while delivering a marathon speech in the Commons lasting three-and-a-half hours, he consumed two bottles of brandy and was apparently every bit as coherent when he finally drew to a close as he had been when he started.

One of the best-known politicians depicted in the square is Winston Churchill (1874–1965). Among the other silent and immobile inhabitants of the square are Abraham Lincoln, Nelson Mandela, David Lloyd George and Mahatma Gandhi.

The east side of the square has witnessed large numbers of political demonstrations over the years; some have been mass gatherings and a few have been by solitary individuals.

On the south side of the square is the church of St Margaret's, Westminster. It is dedicated to St Margaret of Antioch, a virgin and martyr who, we are told, had the misfortune to be swallowed alive by the Devil disguised as a dragon. She survived the trauma only to be beheaded later for her beliefs.

In 1667, Samuel Pepys wrote in his diary that he took his 'perspective glass' to St Margaret's when attending divine service and 'had the pleasure of seeing and gazing at a great many fine women, and sleeping I passed the time away until the sermon was done'.

**Nearest tube:** Westminster, St James's Park.

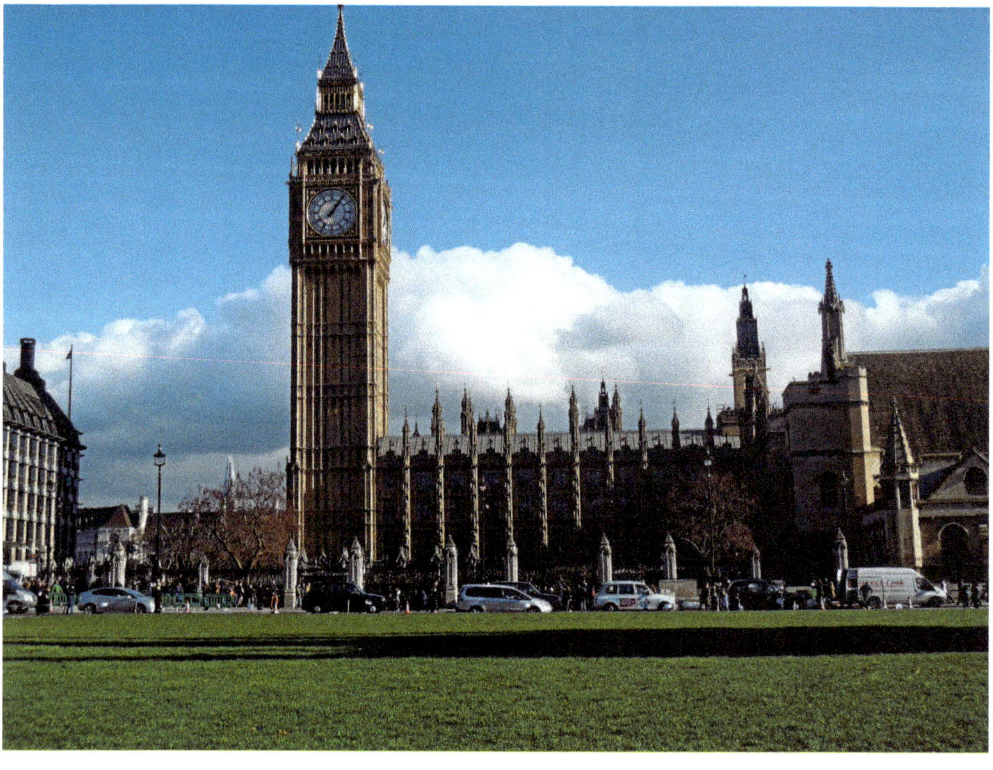

Big Ben with the Shard in the distance in Parliament Square.

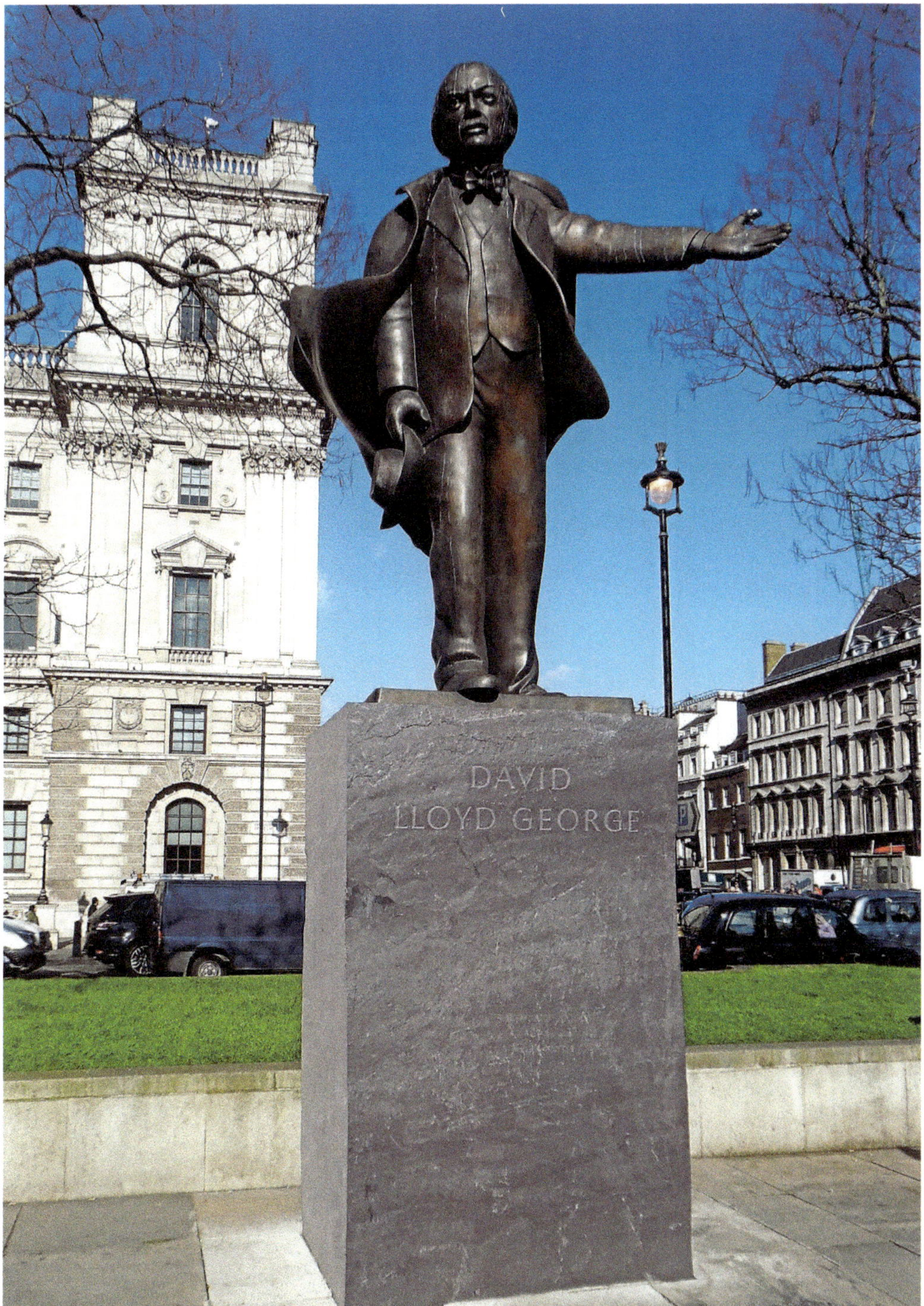


Parliament Square. The statue of David Lloyd George with the Government Offices on Great George Street in the background.

# 17. Pickering Place

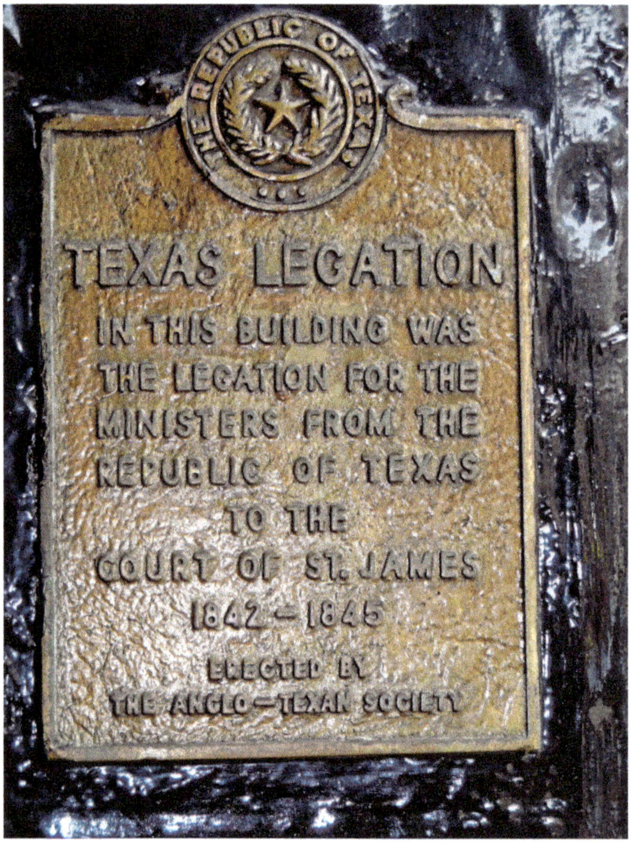


The Texas Legation sign, Pickering Place.

This tiny Georgian square or courtyard is considered to be the smallest public square in London. Despite its size, it has a wealth of history and is well worth seeking out.

In 1731, William Pickering, a successful grocer in St James's Street, entered into a building agreement with the ground landlords that involved demolishing some of the existing buildings and rebuilding the whole property. In 1736, this was described as 'a new Court', then Pickering Court and in 1812 it became Pickering Place.

As you come from Pall Mall into St James's Street, pass Berry Bros & Rudd (thought to be Britain's oldest wine and spirit merchant, established in 1698) and the turning on the right is Pickering Place. The passageway, which has a round-headed archway at the rear as well as on the front, retains its eighteenth-century timber wainscoting. There is a plaque that reads, 'Texas Legation. In this building was the legation for the ministers from the Republic of Texas to the Court of St James 1842–1845.' Texas was once a republic and had its own legation or embassy in London until it ceased to claim its status as an independent country and joined the United States in 1845.

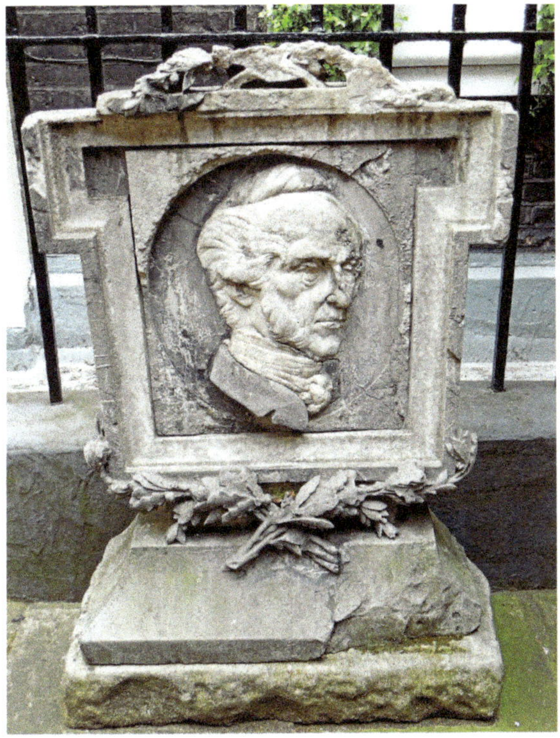

The stone plaque in Pickering Place to Lord Palmerston, Prime Minister in 1855–58 and 1859–1865.

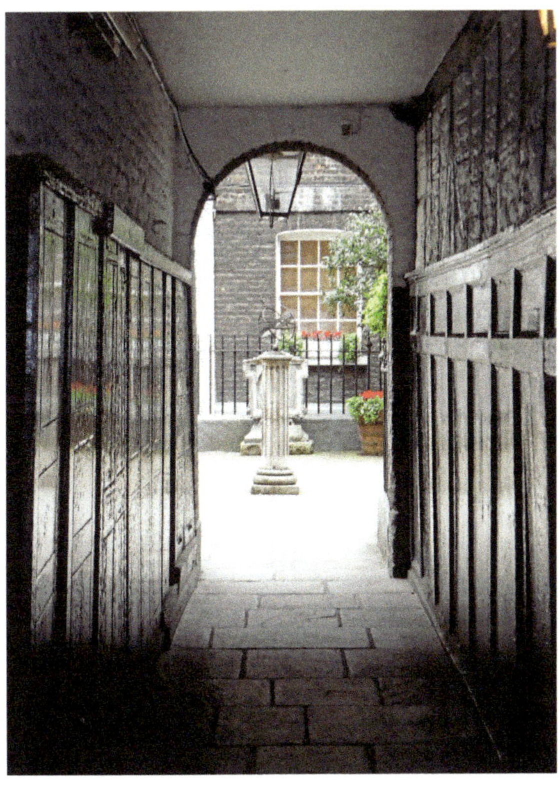

The entrance to Pickering Place.

In the courtyard there is the original Georgian architecture as well as gaslights, a sundial in the centre and a stone plaque commemorating the former Prime Minister Lord Palmerston (1855–58 and 1859–65) who took up residence in the square. The small square is now a place of quiet seclusion although it did have a reputation for its notorious gambling dens, prostitutes, bear-baiting, dogfighting and duels. In 1837, two young men from White's Club took part in what was reputed to be the last duel to the death in London.

Graham Greene, author of *The Third Man* (1951), *Brighton Rock* (1938), The *End of the Affair* (1951), *The Quiet American* (1955) and many more novels, was also a resident of Pickering Place. Beneath the square lies Berry Bros & Rudd's wine cellar.

**Nearest tube:** Green Park.

## 18. Portman Square

Portman Square lies north of Oxford Street in Marylebone. The gardens, which are private, are shaded by London plane trees and also have a lawn, winding paths, informal planting and a tennis court. They also include the Grade II-listed 1878 Hamilton Memorial drinking fountain that was donated by Lady Hamilton through the Drinking Fountain and Cattle Trough Association.

The square, along with nearby Cavendish Square, was built for the wealthy. Sir William Portman, Lord Chief Justice of England, acquired the Portman estate in the mid-sixteenth century. The Portmans were an old established family who owned country estates in Dorset and Somerset. The initiative for the building of the square came from a descendent, Henry William Portman, in 1755, whose vision was to develop over 200 acres of meadow

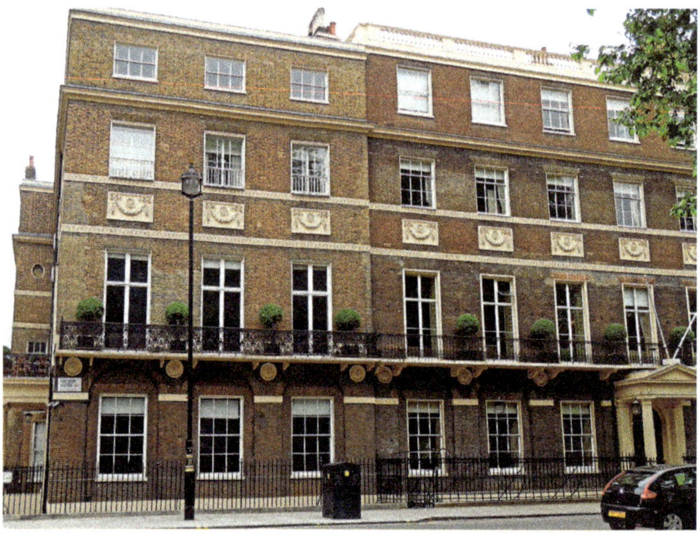

Portman Square's Home House Club.

into one of the grandest residential areas of London. Portman Square would be the nucleus for fashionable houses although it would take at least twenty years before the completion of the project. Development began in the 1750s with Orchard Street and Portman Street, followed by Portman Square between 1764 and 1784.

It was first laid out around 1780 and completely re-landscaped in the early 1900s. The railings and gates were erected in 1882–86, but like many London railings they were removed in 1942 as part of the war effort. They were restored in 1972. The original gates remain with some fine examples of iron overthrow lanterns.

A famous resident was Elizabeth Montagu who became a leading light in the literary world and was the founder of the celebrated Blue Stockings Society, an informal women's social and educational movement in the eighteenth century. Every year, she gave a dinner of roast beef and plum pudding to chimney sweeps and their apprentices. One of the apprentices was David Porter who went on to swap his brushes for the appurtenances of a builder and became extremely wealthy. He later named Montagu Square after her. Elizabeth lived in a house on the north-west corner of Portman Square, built between 1777 and 1782. It was demolished in the Blitz by an incendiary bomb.

Portman Square became a very desirable place to live. William Makepeace Thackeray described the district as 'elegant, prosperous, and the most respectable district of the habitable globe.'

At the north-west corner of Portman Square, at No. 20, Home House was built. Designed by Robert Adam in 1773, the house was built as a palace of entertainment for the Countess of Home. Samuel Courtauld, who established the Courtauld Institute of Art, lived at Home House between 1927 and 1931. Courtauld made over the house in Portman Square, together with the paintings, for the use of the new institute until such a time that permanent accommodation could be found for them. The Portman Square house was to be the institute's home for almost sixty years. The director of the Courtauld Institute between 1947 and 1974 was Anthony Blunt, a distant relative of the Queen and keeper of the royal family's pictures and drawings. In 1963, MI5 discovered that Blunt was a Soviet spy although this remained an official secret until he was publicly named in 1979. Home House now consists of three eighteenth-century town houses, which have been converted into a private members club, the Home House Club.

There are other connections with spying. To the east of Portman Square is Orchard Court. In 1940, Winston Churchill created the Special Operations Executive (SOE) to support resistance movements in Europe. The French or 'F' Section used the flats within Orchard Court and it was here that new spies were recruited. F Section was commanded by Maurice Buckmaster and assisted by Vera Atkins who is said to have been the inspiration for Miss Moneypenny in the James Bond novels by Ian Fleming.

**Nearest tube:** Marble Arch or Bond Street.

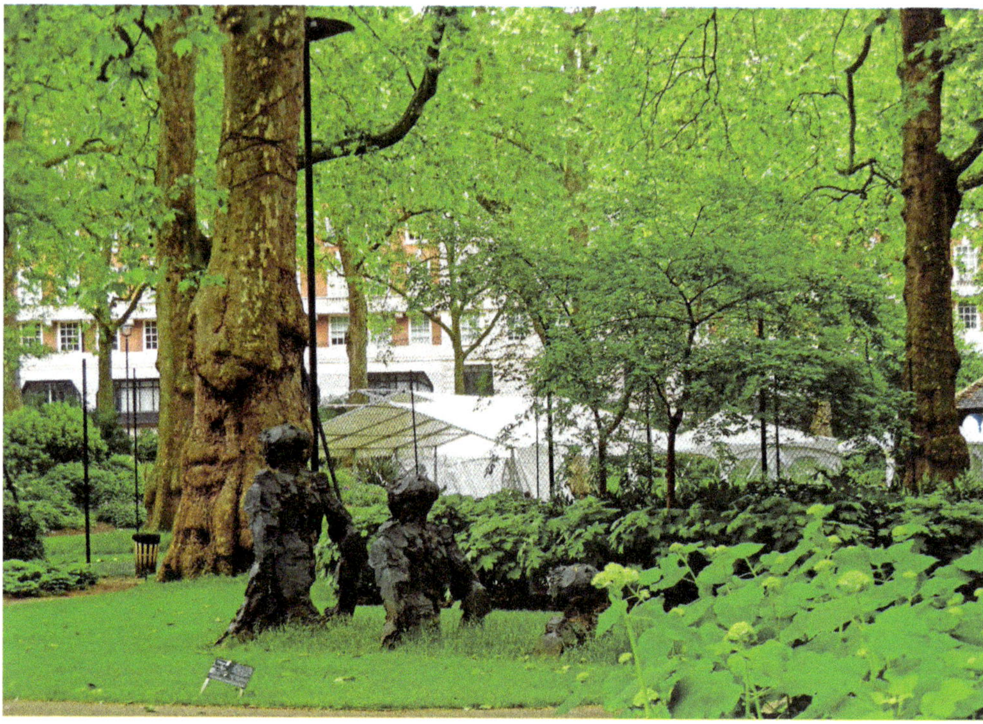

Portman Square Gardens.

# 19. Sloane Square

Sloane Square is a small hard-landscaped square adjacent to the tube station of the same name. The appellation recalls Sir Hans Sloane (1660–1753), an eminent physician, traveller and collector. He founded the Royal Botanical Gardens at Chelsea after having bought Chelsea Manor in 1712. The area was mostly pastureland but it was enclosed and then cobbled from 1771 when residential development began to take place, supervised by Henry Holland. Sloane's extremely large and eclectic collection became a major component of the British Museum.

The Royal Court Theatre stands on the east side of the square. It opened in 1870 in a converted chapel. It was rebuilt and enlarged in 1871 and 1887–88 and became noted for staging the first public performances of several plays by George Bernard Shaw. It closed in 1932, reopened as a cinema in 1934, was destroyed by bombs in 1940 and was rebuilt and reopened as a theatre in 1952. A much-needed refurbishment took place in 1965. Before that, the water closets in the men's toilets flushed so loudly that the noise rendered the actors' voices inaudible for at least two minutes each time the toilet was used. The theatre received a thorough makeover in 2000.

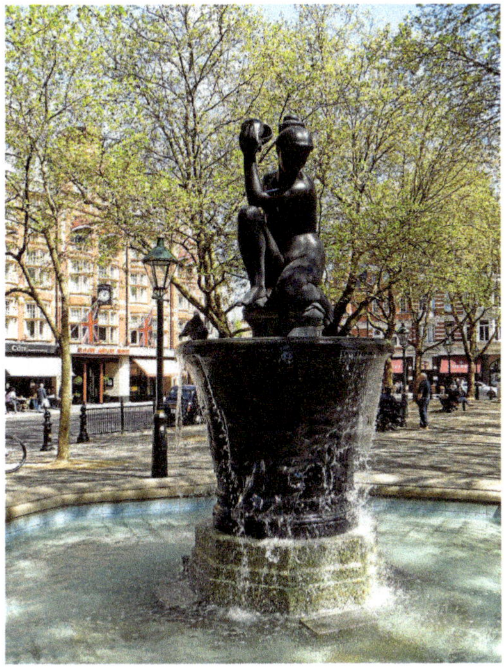

The Venus Fountain, Sloane Square.

A prominent feature of Sloane Square is Peter Jones, the well-known department store, part of the John Lewis Partnership since the early twentieth century. It was founded on this site in 1877 by an enterprising Welshman as a drapery and furnishing store. A new extended building was opened in 1936 and it has come to be regarded as a classic example of the Modernist movement.

The square contains a memorial to the First and Second World Wars and the notable bronze Venus Fountain was unveiled in 1951. Lovers of peace and quiet will find little solace in Sloane Square. It is basically little more than a traffic island around which vehicles hurtle both day and night.

A curiosity of Sloane Square Tube Station is that the stream known as the Westbourne, flowing down from the Serpentine to the Thames, is carried over the track and the platforms in a large, rather inconspicuous iron pipe. On those rare occasions when there is little activity in the station, the unexpected sound of running water can be heard, especially after heavy rain. It says much for the conduit's robust construction that, when the station was wrecked by bombs during the Second World War, it was just about the only thing that emerged unscathed.

'Sloane Rangers' was a term invented in 1975 for young ostentatiously well-to-do, upper-class socialites who supposedly lived mainly in Chelsea and the fashionable parts of Kensington. Lady Diana Spencer, later the Princess of Wales, was something of an archetype 'Sloane'. The concept emerged in printed form in publications such as *The Official Sloane Ranger Handbook* (1982) and *The Official Sloane Ranger Diary* (1983) by Ann Barr.

**Nearest tube:** Sloane Square, Knightsbridge.

# 20. Smith Square

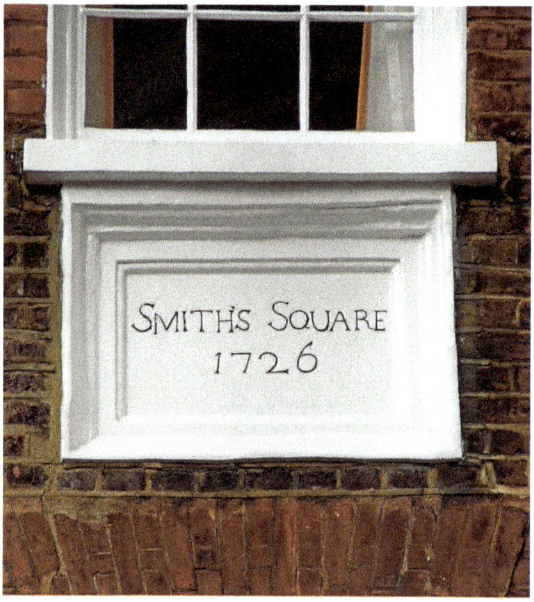


Smith's Square 1726.

Smith Square is just south of the Palace of Westminster and opposite Victoria Tower Gardens on Millbank. Take a short walk down Dean Stanley Street and you will face the magnificent Grade I-listed Baroque church of St John's Smith Square. The square was named after the Smith family, on whose land it was developed in the early eighteenth century. A white plaque above the terraced houses to the north states, 'Smith's Square 1726'. Nos 1–9 on the north side are part of this original development.

The square, unlike most of the other squares covered in this book, has no central garden. It is dominated by the church, which is surrounded by offices mostly occupied by organisations associated with Government, such as Department for Environment, Local Government Association and the London base of the European Parliament and European Commission. Nos 32–34 served as Conservative Central Office headquarters between 1958 and 2003. The old headquarters of the Transport and General Workers Union, the Labour Party and Transport House can still be seen on the south side. It is now Local Government House and a conference centre.

Smith Square was first settled in medieval times, as the Westminster Palace and Abbey complex grew in importance and influence. Testimony to this is a length of medieval wall that remains along Great College Street to the north.

St John's Church was completed in 1728. It is often referred to as 'Queen Anne's Footstool' because, according to legend, when Thomas Archer was designing the church, he asked the Queen what she wanted it to look like. She replied by kicking over her footstool, pointed at its upturned shape and said 'like that', thus giving rise to the building's four

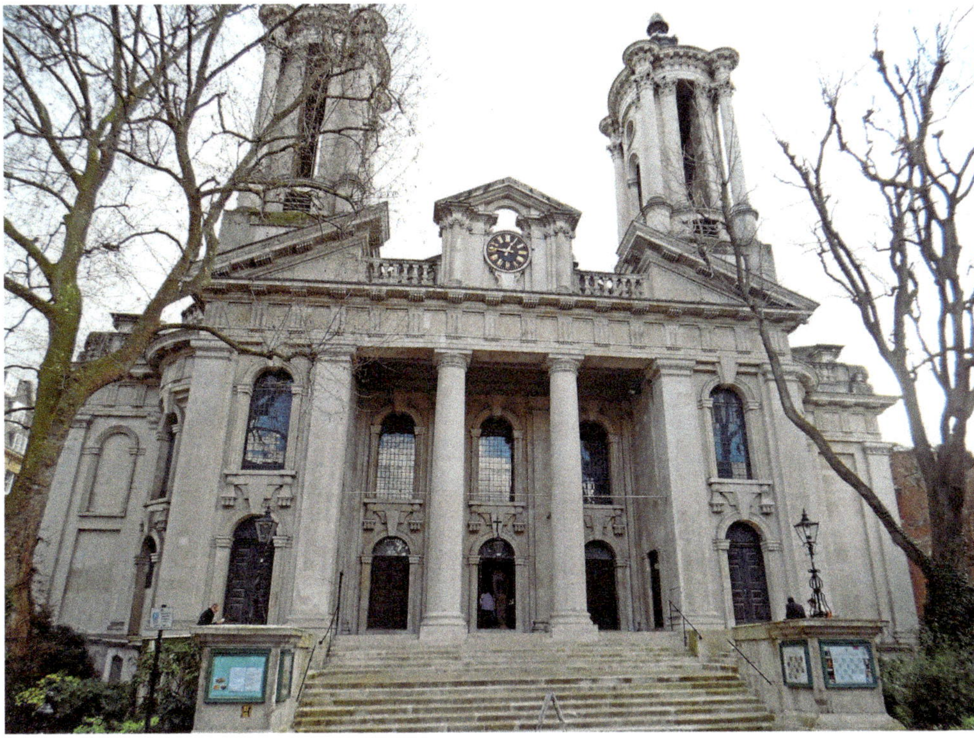

*Above*: St John's Church in Smith Square.

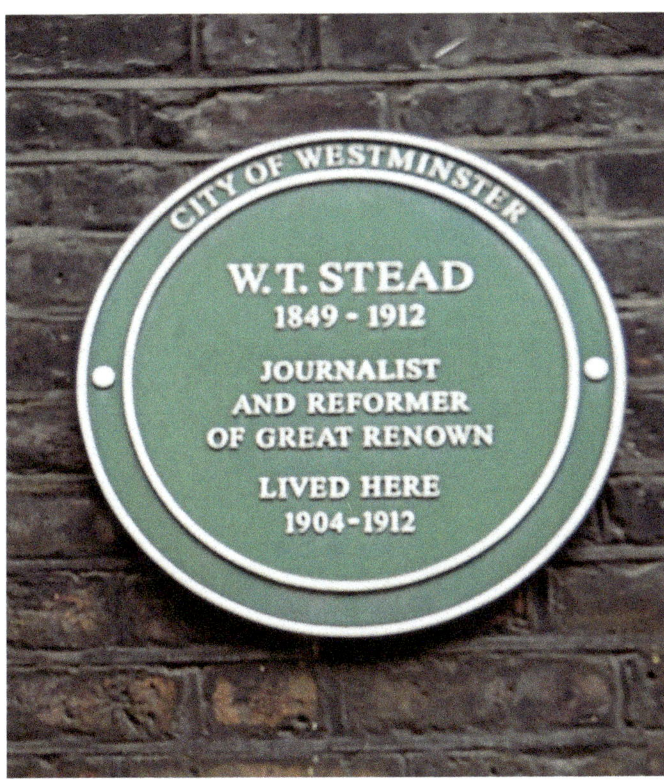


*Right*: A plaque to W. T. Stead, Smith Square.

corner towers. The crypt is now called the Footstool Restaurant. Adjacent to the church are informal mature gardens and large London plane trees.

An Indian chief who died of smallpox in 1734 was buried in St John's Church. He was buried according to the custom of his tribe: 'sewn up in two blankets, between two deal boards, with his clothes, some silver coins, and a few glass beads'.

The church has had its share of misfortune. In 1773, it was struck by lightning and, in 1815, the towers and roof had to be shored up. In May 1941, it was directly hit by an incendiary bomb and gutted by fire during a bombing raid. The church was saved in 1962 and restored by the determination of Lady Parker and Friends of St John's. Since then St John's, Smith Square, has being regarded as one of London's major concert halls.

Smith Square and the surrounding streets have an abundance of listed street furniture. A group of fourteen Grade II-listed nineteenth-century lamp standards with square bases and tulip heads can be seen. In addition, the vicinity of the square is well provided with mid-nineteenth-century railings and basement light wells. At the north side of Smith Square (Lord North Street), there are cast-iron railings with javelin heads. Some properties have foot scrapers set into walls and a relatively common feature are the cast-iron coal-hole covers.

Famous residents include the campaigning journalist William Thomas Stead who lived at No. 5 from 1904 until his death on board the *Titanic* in 1912. Stead became a controversial figure when he published a series of hugely influential articles while editor of the *Pall Mall Gazette* in 1885. The articles exposed an aspect of the world of London vice – stinking brothels, evil procuresses, drugs, and padded rooms, where vicious upper-class rakes could exploit children. As a result, the government was forced to enact the Criminal Law Amendment Act, which, among other things, raised the female age of consent from thirteen to sixteen.

**Nearest tube:** Westminster.

## 21. Soho Square

Soho Square is a short distance south-west of Tottenham Court Road Tube Station. The square was laid out in the 1680s in what was then known as Soho Fields. The unusual word 'Soho' probably had its origins in a hunting cry. The buildings that were put up fairly haphazardly, around what was initially called King Square because it housed a statue of Charles II, were residences of some of London's wealthiest and most fashionable figures. However, its heyday lasted only around a century because, by the 1770s, its most prestigious residents were migrating west to new and exclusive developments, particularly in Mayfair.

Over time, the many premises of Soho were replaced by businesses involved in music, media and communications. The buildings around the square have been rebuilt in random fashion but the centre has remained a sylvan haven much appreciated by local office workers and others. Many free open-air concerts are staged in Soho Square.

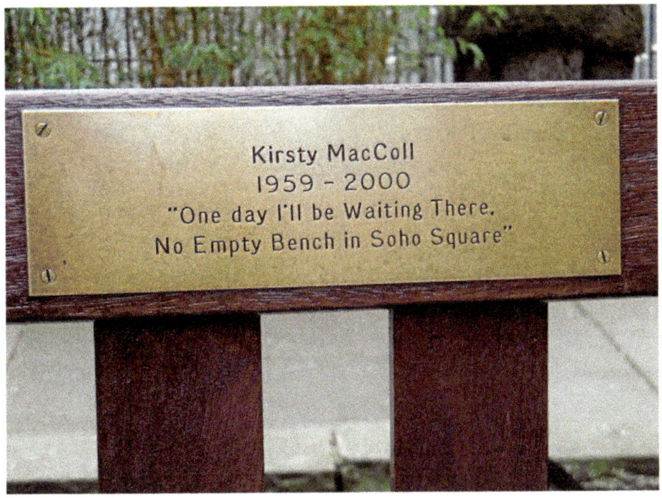


A dedication to Kirsty MacColl in Soho Square.

The marble statue of Charles II (1630–85) was initially erected in 1681. It was removed in 1876 and restored in 1938. Charles was every bit as much a believer in the divine right of kings as was his father who was tried and decapitated by order of Parliament in 1649. Charles II was far more intelligent and pragmatic. He was a bon vivant and enjoyed life to the full, fathering innumerable children by a wide range of lovers. A contemporary description of him was 'A prince of many Virtues, and many greater Imperfections, Debonair, Easy of Accesse, not bloody or Cruel.' He became known as the 'Merry Monarch'.

The famous botanist Joseph Banks was born at No. 32 in 1743 and William Beckford at No. 22 in 1760. Beckford inherited a vast fortune from his father's plantations, which gave him the entry to high society. At the age of nineteen, William fell desperately in love with the eleven-year-old William Courtenay, 9th Earl of Devon. Beckford decided to travel abroad until the furore died down.

No. 19 was occupied in 1836 by Messrs Burroughes and Watts, manufacturers of billiard balls. Hunting creatures to obtain ivory was not an issue in those days and around 1,000 elephants were slaughtered every year in order to provide the raw material for the company's business.

Carlisle House formerly stood on the east side of the square on the site of the present Roman Catholic Church of St Patrick, the first church in England to be dedicated to this saint. In the 1760s, this was used as assembly rooms and some extremely wild parties took place there. At one of these, Joseph Merlin, who regularly attended such events and who was the inventor of the roller skate, hurtled through the closely packed crowd on his skates while also playing the violin. He got out of control and crashed into a very large, ornate mirror, shattering it. He was apparently unhurt but he caused damage amounting to £500.

A sign that reads 'House of Charity' can be seen from the gardens. This is the House of St Barnabas, a Grade I-listed building noted for its rococo plasterwork and architectural features. Since 1862, the house has been run as a charity to help the homeless. The name was changed from the House of Charity to the House of St Barnabas in 1951.

Near to the southern entrance to the gardens, there is a memorial bench to Kirsty MacColl (1959–2000), the British singer and songwriter who was the daughter of the well-known

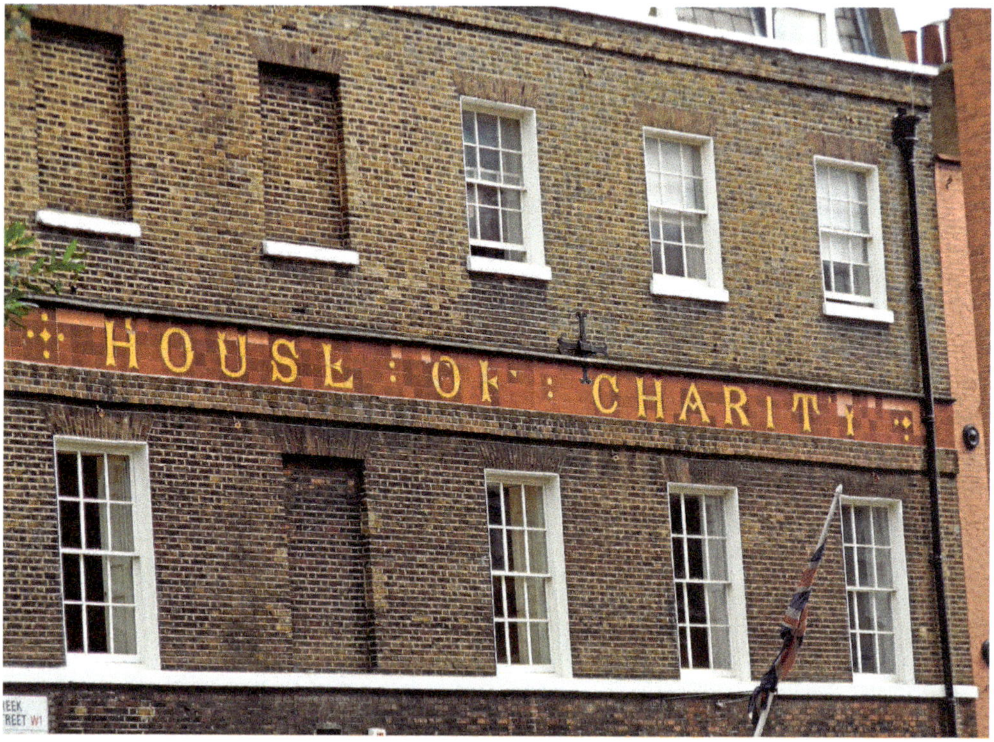


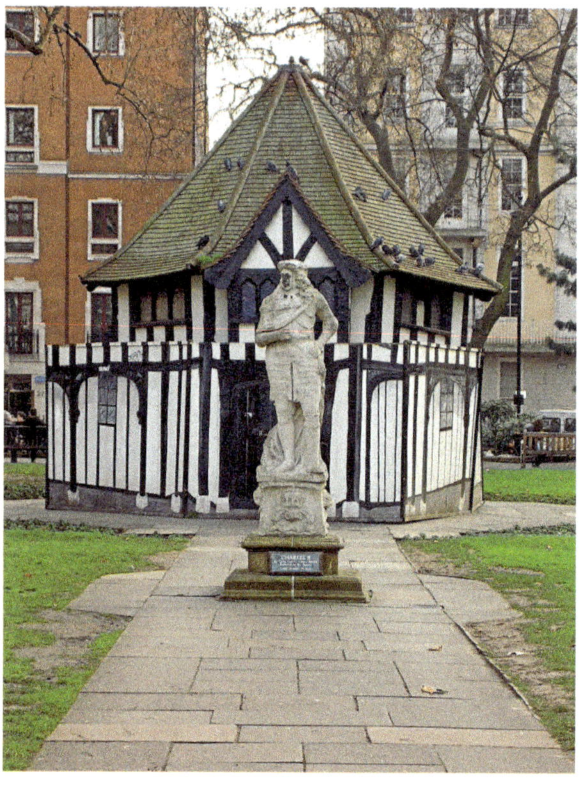

*Above*: The House of Charity sign, Soho Square.

*Left*: The statue of Charles II in front of the tool shed in Soho Square.

folk singer Ewan MacColl. The bench was placed there in 2001 and the inscription evokes a lyric from one of her most poignant songs: 'One day I'll be waiting there / No empty bench in Soho Square'.

The famous mock-Tudor half-timbered 'tool shed' was built in 1895 and is used by those who maintain the gardens. It is said to have once housed a transformer of the Charing Cross Electric Light Company. Beneath the square, air-raid shelters were built during the Second World War.

**Nearest tube:** Leicester Square, Tottenham Court Road, Oxford Circus.

## 22. St Anne's Churchyard Gardens

St Anne's Gardens have a real sense of character and provide a pleasant haven in the middle of Soho. The gardens are located on Wardour Street just off Shaftesbury Avenue.

The parish was dedicated to St Anne because Bishop Henry Compton, who consecrated the church in 1686, had been tutor to Princess Anne before she became Queen. It was formerly the churchyard of St Anne's, Soho, but was closed to burials in 1853. It is estimated that there were over 100,000 burials within the churchyard. Such was the need to bury the dead in the early nineteenth century that the church gardens were raised 2 metres above the pavement to accommodate a further 10,000 corpses.

The original church and churchyard date from 1686. The Metropolitan Public Gardens Association laid out the churchyard as a public garden in 1891. St Anne's, a Christopher

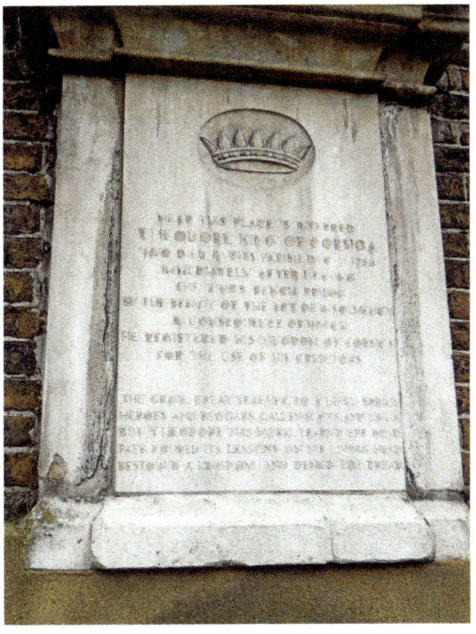

The plaque to the King of Corsica (d. 1756).

Wren church, was destroyed by bombs in the Second World War and was reopened in 1991, thanks to the efforts of The Soho Society. It was incorporated into a new development of offices and housing association flats. The old church tower stands as the main ornament in this small park.

The demand for experimenting on fresh corpses during the eighteenth and nineteenth centuries prompted the growth of bodysnatching and the notorious St Anne's churchyard, like many others, fell victim to such foul deeds. In February 1806, *The Times* reported that resurrection men, armed with grapplers and pickaxes, were apprehended on this site. Five of the gang of six got away. The body of a woman and child were found in the ground 'in a state' of being 'carried away'. In 1839, George Walker, a London surgeon who carried out a survey of the city's overcrowded cemeteries, wrote of what he saw in St Anne's churchyard: '... you may see human heads, covered with hair; and here ... are human heads with flesh still adhering to them ...'

The churchyard has various gravestones, plaques and memorials, including one to writer, painter and philosopher William Hazlitt who was buried there in 1830 and Theodore Etienne, King of Corsica (d. 1756). There is a memorial to the victims of the Admiral Duncan bombing in which two people were killed and thirty injured in a nail bomb attack on the Soho pub in 1999. The ashes of Dorothy L. Sayers, the crime writer, are buried beneath the tower in the square. In 2007, a small 'toilet pod' was installed which doubles as a mini local museum.

The clock in the church tower is still wound by hand and is the only remaining part of the old church that was bombed in the Blitz of 1940.

**Nearest tube:** Piccadilly Circus.

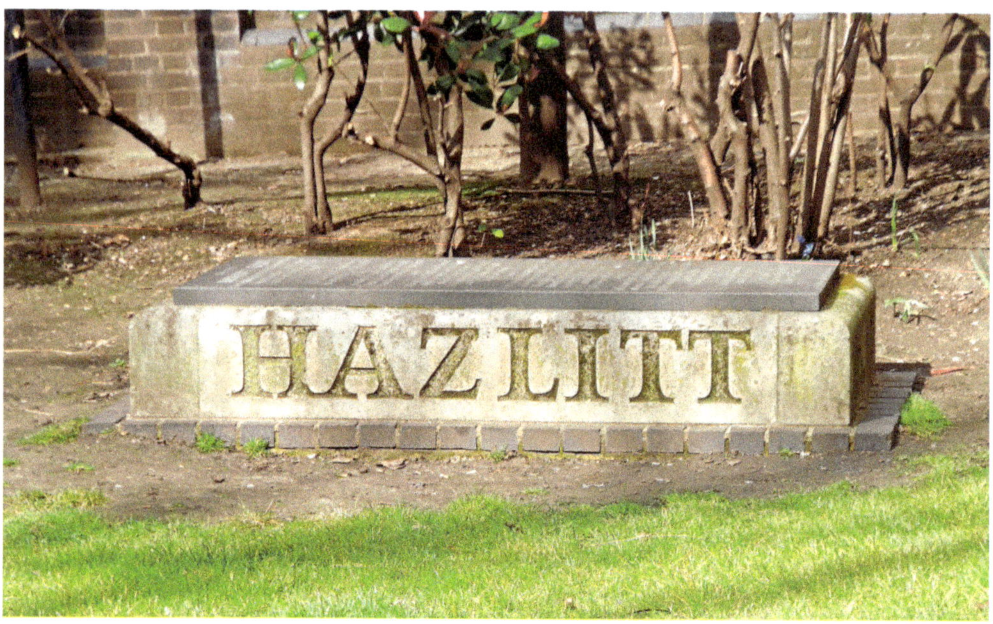


St Anne's churchyard gardens is the burial place of William Hazlitt.

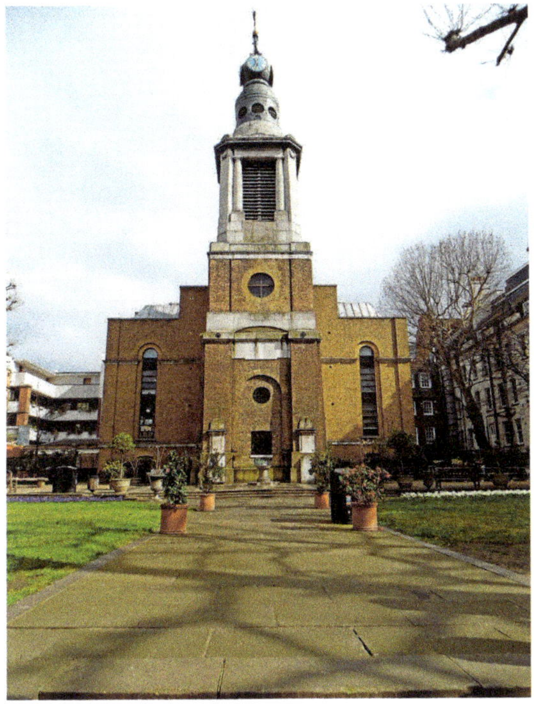

St Anne's churchyard gardens.

## 23. St James's Square

In his *Handbook to London* (1862), George Bradshaw described St James's Square as 'the most fashionable in London'. This is not surprising given that St James's has the highest concentration of listed buildings in England, with nearly sixty Grade I- and Grade II-listed buildings. The square is located just north of Pall Mall and south of Piccadilly Tube Station. It is a very pleasant square with a diverse range of flowers and shrubbery and is worth seeking out.

St James's Square was one of the first of the West End squares. In 1662, Henry Jermyn, 1st Earl of St Albans, was given an extension to his lease over the 45 acres of Pall Mall from Charles II. Jermyn, described as 'a man of pleasure', seemed well suited to build a garden square designed to house London's wealthiest families. This represented one of the first major shifts westwards for the nobility and court followers after the disasters of fire and plague in the City of London. In 1665, the king granted the freehold of the site of St James's Square, which made the location convenient for the royal palaces of Whitehall and St James's. Jermyn's intended air of grandeur was realised when seven dukes and seven earls were in residence in the square. St James's Square was enclosed in 1663 and the garden square railings were added in 1727. There is a green plaque to Henry Jermyn at No. 10 St James's Square, the house where he died in 1684.

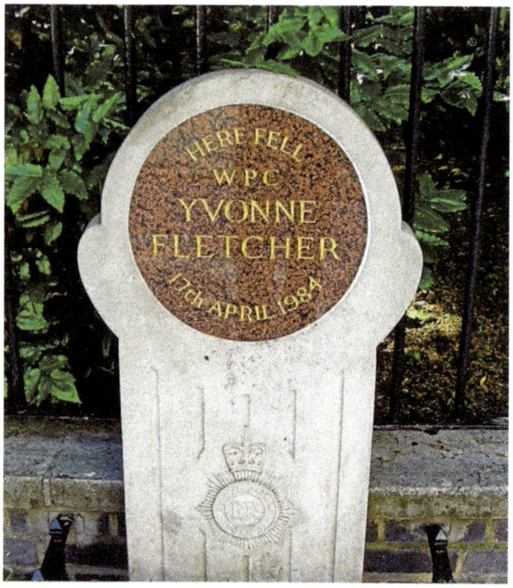


St James's Square memorial to Yvonne Fletcher.

St James's is derived from the dedication of a twelfth-century leper hospital to St James the Less. St James's Palace now occupies the site of the hospital. The square is built on the site of the old St James's Fields and the surrounding streets were named after Charles II and his royal brother, the Duke of York (afterwards James II) – namely, King Street, Charles Street, Duke Street, and York Street.

However, by the late eighteenth century, most of the houses had been rebuilt or extensively redesigned. Over the next 100 years, as fashionable London moved to Belgravia, tradesmen and clubs moved in around St James's Square. During the nineteenth century, the square formed the focus for the development of gentlemen's clubs.

Little of the original fabric of the square's buildings remain as they were taken over by commercial or institutional interests. The gardens were gradually opened to the public from 1933 onwards. By the Second World War, the number of private houses had diminished to three or four and now it is almost entirely commercial.

One of the clubs in St James's Square is the East India Club at No. 16. Founded in 1849, its original members were the servants of the East India Company and commissioned officers of Her Majesty's Army and Navy.

The gardens host a collection of mature trees, a prevalence of listed street lamps, link extinguishers outside Ormond House on the north side of the square, a statue of William III erected in 1808 as a focal point in the centre and a plaque to Nancy Astor (1879–1964), the first woman to sit in parliament, who lived at No. 4. A memorial plaque to WPC Yvonne Joyce Fletcher (1958–84), who was shot during a protest outside the Libyan Embassy in 1984, stands in the north-east corner of the square and a memorial tree to her has also been planted in the gardens. Her death resulted in the Metropolitan Police Force laying siege to the embassy for eleven days. No one has yet been convicted for her murder.

In the north-west corner of the square, at No. 14, is the London Library, which dates from 1896, founded by the historian Thomas Carlyle and others. It was a response in disgust to the inefficiency of the British Library. The impressive collection contains over a million volumes, making it the world's largest independent lending library. Past members reads like a who's who of British literary icons: Sir Arthur Conan Doyle, Kingsley Amis, Winston Churchill, John Betjeman, Agatha Christie, Charles Dickens, Rudyard Kipling and Virginia Woolf were members and T. S. Eliot was the library's president from 1952 to 1965. The library is open to everyone for a fee and still follows its own original rule to never discard any book, no matter how unfashionable it becomes.

St James's Square has had many famous residents including architect Robert Adam, three prime ministers (William Pitt the Elder, Edward Smith-Stanley, 14th Earl of Derby, and William Gladstone) and, during the Second World War, both Generals Eisenhower and de Gaulle had headquarters here.

Foreign Secretary Lord Castlereagh resided at No. 16 in 1813. Castlereagh, never a popular figure, had his house attacked by an angry mob in 1816. He also invited biting words from two of England's most famous poets, Byron and Shelley. In his poem *The Mask of Anarchy* (written in 1819 as a response to the Peterloo Massacre where fifteen people were killed by the cavalry while attending a peaceful gathering), Percy Bysshe Shelley wrote, 'I met Murder on the way - He had a mask like Castlereagh.'

Ada, Countess of Lovelace (1815–52), was a British mathematician and writer but is mostly known for her work on Charles Babbage's mechanical computer. She is often regarded as the first computer programmer, a contribution that has been honoured by the British Computer Society who awarded a medal in her name in 1998 and in 2008 initiated an annual competition for female students of computer science. A blue plaque commemorates where she lived, at No. 12.

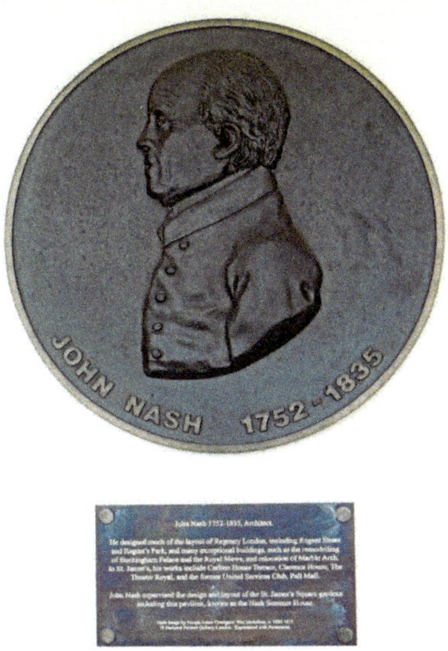


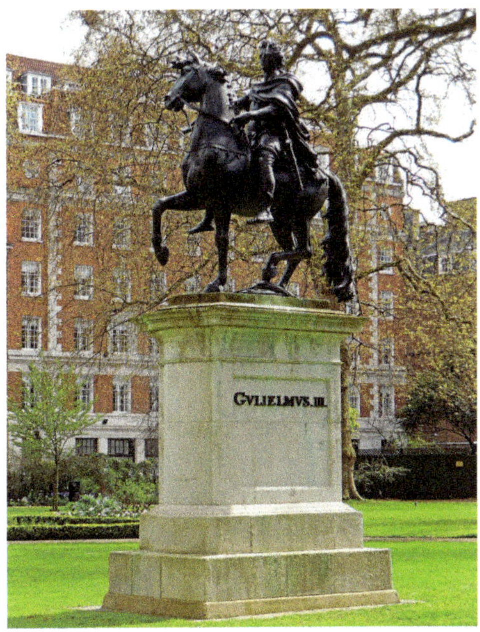


*Above left*: The plaque to John Nash in St James's Square Gardens.

*Above right*: The statue of William III, St James's Square Gardens.

John Nash (1752–1835), a British architect, supervised and designed St James's Square's gardens including the pavilion where there is a plaque dedicated to him. He was also responsible for most of the layout of Regency London. His best-known buildings are the Royal Pavilion in Brighton and Buckingham Palace.

Brothels were common in London and particularly the West End. Henry Mayhew noted that 'we cannot have a better example of this sort of thing than the bawdy-houses in King's Place, St James's'. King's Place was an alley off King Street, west of St James's Square. Even with the exclusive male clubs around St James's Square, brothels catered for the pleasures of the aristocracy and the well-to-do. So well organised were some of these 'nunneries' that they could employ surgeons to inspect the prostitutes.

**Nearest tube:** Piccadilly Circus.

# 24. St John's Gardens

St John's Gardens is a small but perfectly formed garden west of Millbank along Horseferry Road. It was the former burial ground of St John's Smith Square. St John's soon became overcrowded and an extension was acquired in 1823 but it later closed to burials in 1853. The former burial ground was laid out as a public garden and opened in 1885.

Many of the old gravestones were stacked against the perimeter. The garden is surrounded by railings and contains a number of high trees, flower beds, an impressive fountain and a smattering of benches which provide a retreat for nearby workers.

It was once London's cheapest burial ground, accommodating tramps, prostitutes and the impoverished. Not surprisingly, it became filled to its capacity within twenty years. One report said that over 5,000 graves had been dug in ten years. The graveyard suffered from the activities of bodysnatchers and two watchmen were appointed for night duty in 1781 in order to protect the bodies from the fate of dissection in the anatomy theatre. As a response to the problem of overcrowding, 3 feet of earth was deposited over the whole area and this explains why today's gardens are now a few feet higher than the area around them.

The beautiful building next door is the former Westminster Hospital, which we can assume allowed for an easy exit for patients that sadly died. The land between Horseferry Road and Vauxhall Bridge Road was also the site of the huge Millbank Prison, which opened as a model prison in the early nineteenth century. When this finally closed in 1890, Tate Britain was built on part of the old site.

In 1853, Lord Palmerston closed the burial ground, claiming it had become a great public nuisance. After some thirty years of neglect, it was converted into a public garden.

**Nearest tube:** Westminster, St James's Park.

# 25. St Paul's Churchyard, Covent Garden

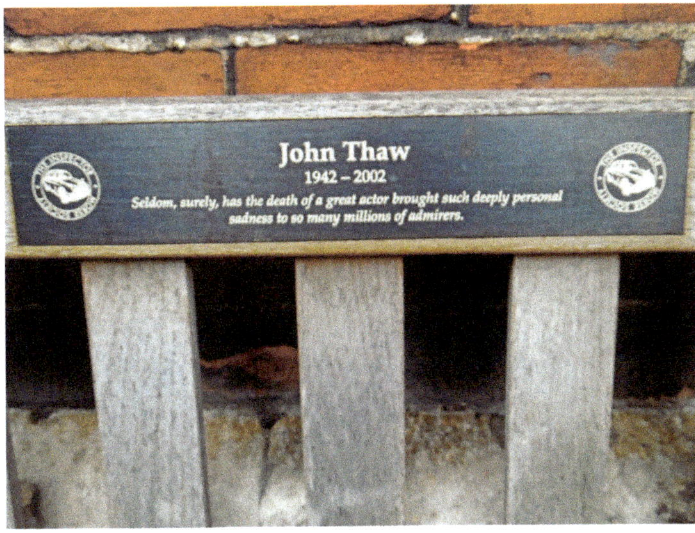


A dedication to John Thaw in St Paul's churchyard.

It is easy to miss this fascinating churchyard amid the bustle of Covent Garden. Situated behind St Paul's Church, it offers a number of interesting attractions for the visitor.

The design of the church and accompanying churchyard was attributed to Inigo Jones and completed in 1633. Three years earlier, the 4th Earl of Bedford had been given permission to develop land he owned north of the Strand; the result was the Covent Garden Piazza, the first formal square in London. St Paul's Church was the first entirely new church to be built in London since the Reformation. The first known victim of the 1665–66 outbreak of the plague in England, Margaret Ponteous, was buried in the churchyard on 12 April 1665. The artist J. M. W. Turner and dramatist Sir William S. Gilbert of Gilbert and Sullivan fame were both baptized at St Paul's. Thomas Arne, who composed 'Rule Britannia' was baptised and buried here.

The church is known as 'the actor's church' because of its association with the theatre. The connection with the theatre began as early as 1663 with the establishment of the Theatre Royal, Drury Lane, and was further assured in 1723 with the opening of Covent Garden Theatre, now the Royal Opera House. In May 1662, Samuel Pepys noted the first 'Italian puppet play' under the portico, which was the first recorded performance of Punch and Judy.

The graveyard originally surrounded the church on three sides. In 1853, the ground was closed to burials, following the Burial Act of that year and, in 1855, the tombstones were removed or laid flat. On the north-east entrance to the church stands a statue, *The Conversion of St Paul*, by Bruce Denny in 2010, which was unveiled by Dame Judy Dench in March 2015.

The benches in the churchyard have dedications to people associated with the acting profession. These vary from well-known performers such as Beryl Reid and John Thaw, who played the lead role in the *Inspector Morse* television series, to those lesser-known performers such as Leslie David Crawford (1933–2006), the actor and stuntman who was 'valiant to the very end'.

There are a number of old street lamps in the churchyard as well as blue plaque on a railing which reads, 'This Lightwell is part of the burial ground of St Paul's Church. Written consent must be obtained before any use can be made of this lightwell.' A light well or air-shaft is an open area or vertical shaft in the centre of a building, often roofed with glass, bringing natural light or ventilation to the lower floors or basement.

**Nearest tube:** Covent Garden.

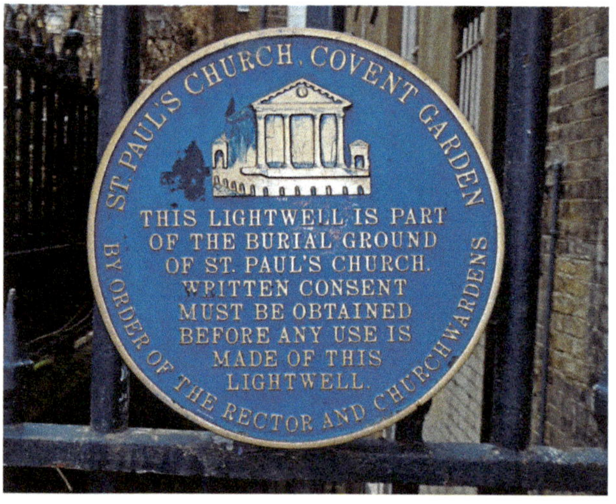


The sign for the light well in St Paul's churchyard.

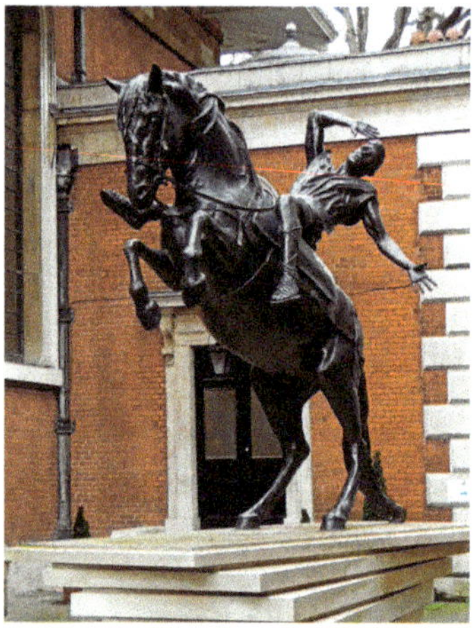

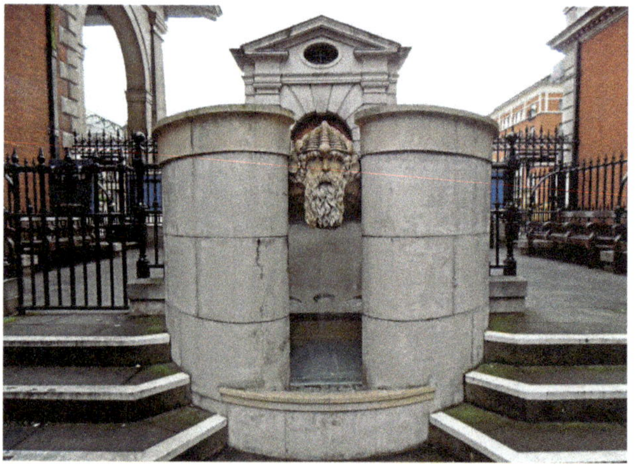

*Above left*: *The Conversion of St Paul*, by Bruce Denny, 2010.

*Above right*: The fountain in St Paul's churchyard.

# 26. Trafalgar Square

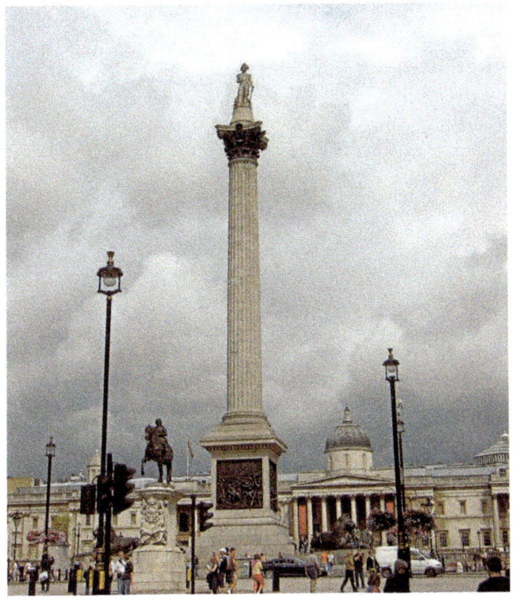


The square, which is opposite Charing Cross Tube Station, was built as a spatial war memorial between 1829 and 1841. It was given the name 'Trafalgar' around 1835. It was built on a sloping site close to that part of London then known as Charing Cross. This cross was one of twelve erected in 1290 on the orders of Edward I. They were located at those places where the cortège carrying the body of his deceased wife, Eleanor, stopped overnight on its journey from Harby, near Lincoln, to Westminster for the interment. The original was demolished in the middle of the seventeenth century and a replica unveiled in 1863, which can be seen close to Charing Cross Station. Only three of the original crosses survive virtually intact.

Nelson's Column is clearly one of Britain's most iconic sights. It is 51 metres high and the figure of Nelson himself is 5 metres in height. This figure was made in two parts that were joined together when they were raised to the top of the column in 1843. The statue was widely criticised at the time as being a very poor representation of Nelson, but the authorities were not unduly concerned, arguing that, with its height, it was unlikely that, once it was erected, anyone would be able to get a close look at it.

Horatio Nelson (1758–1815) is arguably the nation's greatest naval commander. He is shown in an admiral's full-dress uniform. The column is composed of granite and there was no sense of urgency in completing it and its accessories. Work commenced in 1840, the panels around the base were fixed between 1849 and 1852 and the lions, with seeming reluctance, did not put in an appearance until 1867. These were the work of Sir Henry Landseer, the notable animal painter. The bronze bas-reliefs on the side of the pedestal were cast from melted-down captured French naval cannons or the wreck of the *Royal George* depending on which version you choose to believe. They represent incidents during the Battles of St Vincent, the Nile, Copenhagen and Trafalgar, these being Nelson's greatest successes.

On the west side of the column, there is damage to the base, done by Dominion troops in 1918 celebrating victory in the First World War. They commandeered a watchman's hut, poured oil over it and set it on fire. The four lions guarding the base of the column were long known as 'the postman's friend'. This is because, over the years, large numbers of letters have been sent addressed to 'Lord Nelson, Trafalgar Square'. They were usually returned to sender marked 'Unable to deliver. Four large lions guarding'. The lions were cast by the famous sculptor Baron Marochetti. Four days before the statue was completed, a group of fourteen stonemasons had a celebratory rump steak dinner on the top of the column.

There is a large amount of statuary in the square. In front of the column is an equestrian statue of Charles I facing down Whitehall, ironically in the direction of the place of his execution. Close by stands a representation of Charles Napier (1782–1853), the famous soldier, which was unveiled in 1855. This was widely criticised at the time for looking nothing like him. He was very short-sighted but the statue does not show him with the spectacles that he had to wear at all times nor does it do justice to his famously enormous nose and the huge bushy beard with which he was always associated.

Almost a twin of the Napier statue is that of the prominent soldier Henry Havelock (1795–1857). He is little known now but helped to suppress the so-called Indian Mutiny, aka The Indian Rebellion, in 1857, which he did with brutal savagery. This statue is of note as the first statue to be modelled based on photographs of the subject. Havelock is now largely forgotten but there is a certain irony in that Havelock was a leading teetotaller but the sculptor of the work, William Behnes, was found drunk and totally incapable in the street a few years later and he died shortly afterwards.

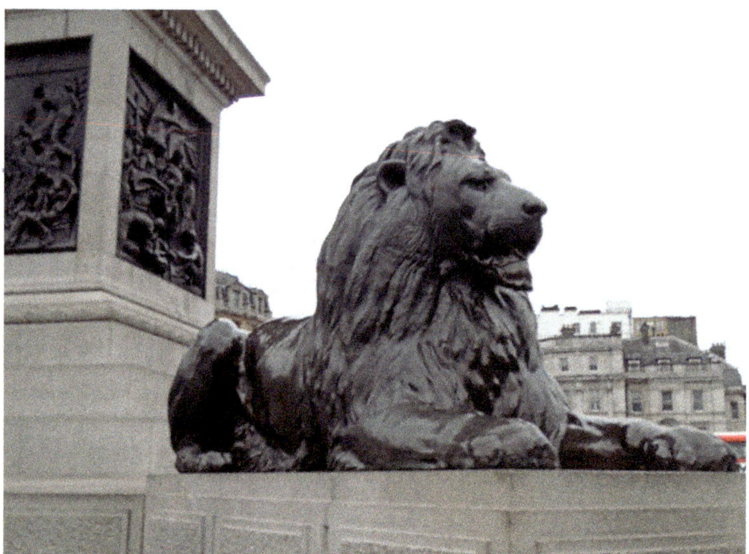

A lion at the base of Nelson's Column in Trafalgar Square.

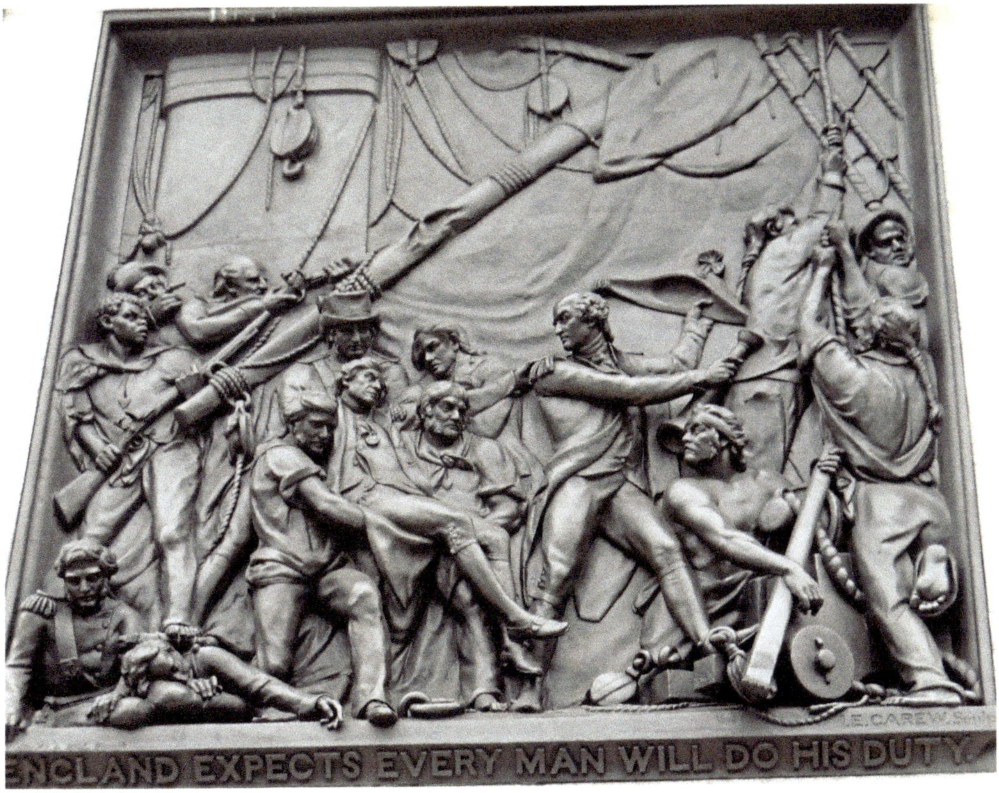


The death of Nelson. One of four bronze bas-reliefs at the base of the column.

An equestrian statue of George IV, erected in 1843, shows a well-proportioned king astride the horse rather than the grossly obese and gout-ridden creature he became. Curiously, the king is apparently riding his horse bareback. There is a statue of James II, probably one of the country's least popular monarchs, zealously determined to return England to the Catholic fold despite the wishes of the majority of its citizens. In the north-west corner, a plinth was built intended to form the base for a statue of William IV. This statue was never made and the plinth lay unused although, more recently, it has provided the base for temporary displays of modern sculptures.

In front of the National Gallery stands a statue of George Washington (1732–99), the leader of the rebels in the American War of Independence. It was unveiled in 1921. Among the other items to be seen in the square are the granite fountains originally brought into use in 1845 and remodelled several times since.

A plaque at the corner of the Strand and Charing Cross Road indicates that it is the central point of London from which all distances in the UK are measured. Busts of the twentieth-century British Admirals of the Fleet – Cunningham, Beatty and Jellicoe – can be seen. There are drinking fountains donated by the delightfully named Metropolitan Drinking Fountain and Cattle Trough Association. A well-known eccentricity at the south-east corner of the square is a tiny police communications kiosk basically contained inside a lamp post. If it is accepted as being a police station, it is the smallest in Britain.

It was built to monitor marches and demonstrations held in the square. It could just about house an average-sized police officer and it had direct telephone communication with Scotland Yard.

Close to the east side of the square stands St Martin's-in-the-Fields. It was consecrated in 1726 and is perhaps the best-known example of the work of the Scottish architect James Gibbs. It is one of London's best-loved churches and is in constant use, not just for worship but for all manner of meetings, concerts and charitable work with the homeless. Among those christened here are Francis Bacon, the scientist who died in 1561, Charles II, Nell Gwynne, who was buried in 1687, Jack Sheppard, the notorious highwayman and escapologist (d.1724), William Hogarth, the satirical engraver (d.1764), the artist Sir Joshua Reynolds (d.1792) and Thomas Chippendale, the cabinetmaker who died in 1779. On 1 June 1727, an Italian called Violante slid down a rope suspended from the spire of St Martin's. He covered a distance of 300 yards from the spire to the far side of what is now Trafalgar Square.

The National Gallery, founded in 1824, stands prominently to the north of the square and houses a large collection of famous paintings dating from the thirteenth century to the nineteenth century and includes artists such as Botticelli, Leonardo da Vinci, Rembrandt, Gainsborough, Turner, Renoir, Cezanne and Van Gogh. The present building, the third to house the National Gallery, was designed by William Wilkins from 1832 to 1838. To the west is the Sainsbury Wing, an extension to the gallery designed by Robert Venturi and Denise Scott Brown, built in 1991.

Trafalgar Square has had a long history of being the gathering place for political meetings and demonstrations. The largest political demonstration ever seen in Britain was the 'Stop the War' march on 15 February 2003, protesting against the armed intervention in Iraq. A large proportion of the estimated 2 million participants managed to squeeze into the square on that occasion.

**Nearest tubes:** Embankment, Charing Cross.

# 27. Victoria Embankment Gardens

These gardens are located next to Embankment Tube Station. The gardens are usually busy but they represent what is best about London's public squares where people can find a pleasant and peaceful space surrounded by beautiful flowers and greenery.

The gardens were created in 1865 by Sir Joseph Bazalgette as part of his extensive embanking work on this side of the Thames. The gardens were designed and laid out a few years later on land recovered from the Thames on both sides of Charing Cross Bridge and are a relatively secluded magnet for office workers and tourists, particularly in fine weather. They contain many commemorative statues of which the following are a small sample.

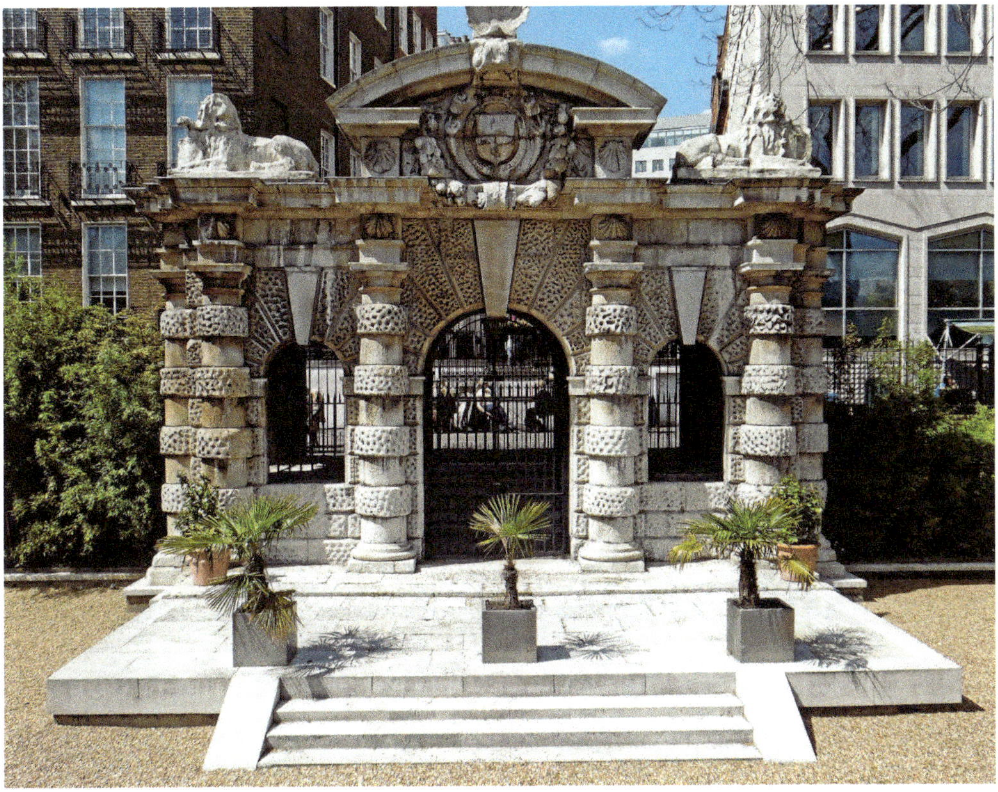

York Watergate in Victoria Embankment Gardens.

John Stuart Mill (1806–73), the radical journalist and political philosopher, was an MP from 1865–68 and the first parliamentarian to bring a motion to the House of Commons proposing votes for women. It was howled down with derision.

Isambard Kingdom Brunel (1806–59) was a remarkable figure who could turn his hand to mechanical, civil and marine engineering and was extraordinarily innovative and typified the grandiloquent confidence of the British at the height of their domination of the world. For all that, he was something of a flawed genius and by no means did all his projects generate profits for those that invested in them.

William Tyndale (*c.* 1495–1536) translated the Bible into everyday English. The invention of the printing press enabled Bibles to be produced far more cheaply. He believed that ordinary people should have access to what he thought of as the 'Word of God' rather than having it 'explained' by a priest. He was opposed by the Church and paid for his beliefs by being executed for heresy.

Robert Burns (1759–96) is generally recognised as Scotland's national bard but is acclaimed throughout the world. Part of his continuing popularity is probably because he was a man of humble origins who expressed, in words, ideas with which ordinary people could relate. A great womaniser and, when drinking, something of a hellraiser, it is quite possible that he would not have wanted the posthumous tribute represented by a statue near the 'Mother of Parliaments'.

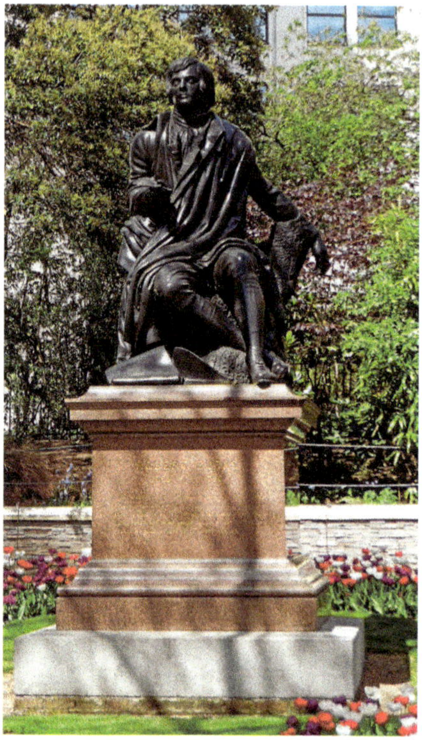

The statue of Robert Burns.

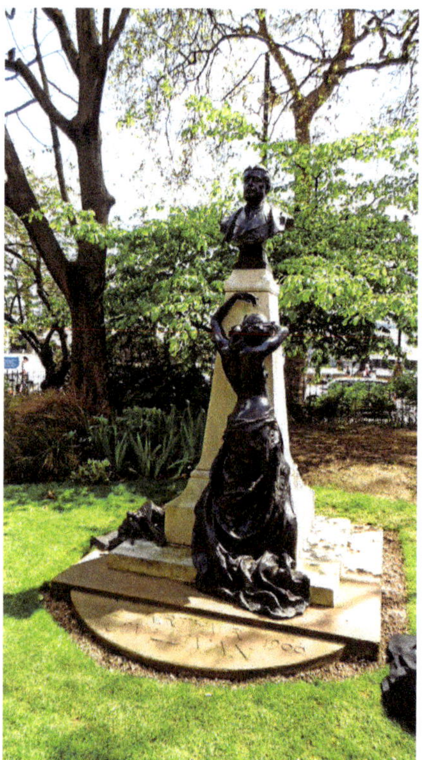

The bust of Sir Arthur Sullivan (of Gilbert and Sullivan fame) with a naked woman representing music.

East of Charing Cross stands the York Watergate. This was built in 1626 to give access to the Thames for the Duke of Buckingham who owned much of the land. The gate is in its original position well away from the river and provides evidence of the extent to which the course of the Thames has been narrowed over time as it passes through London.

The best-known landmark on Victoria Embankment is the Egyptian obelisk better known as Cleopatra's Needle. This dates from *c.*1450 BC. It is the oldest monument in London and was presented to George IV by the British Viceroy in Egypt. It was not, however transported to Britain, erected and unveiled until 1878. It is believed that it was intended to commemorate Britain's eventual defeat of Napoleon and particularly Nelson's outstanding victory at the Battle of Aboukir Bay. Its seaborne passage to Britain was challenging and resulted in several deaths, some people claiming that a curse is attached to it. Two Victorian bronze sphinxes were added to it although they should be guarding it by looking at and not away from it. Its history is outlined on the base. Damage from air raids can also be seen.

**Nearest tube:** Embankment.

## 28. Victoria Tower Gardens

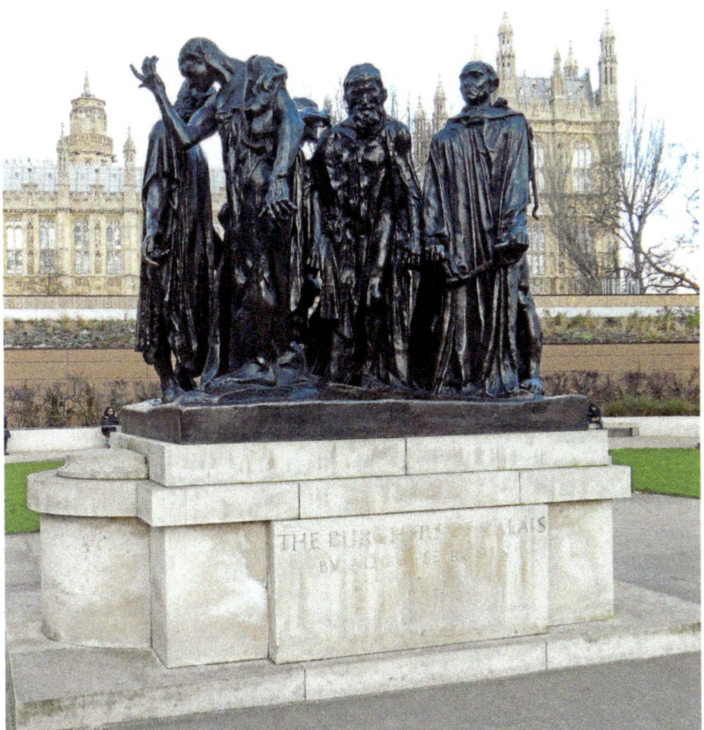

*The Burghers of Calais* by Auguste Rodin in Victoria Tower Gardens.

The triangular-shaped Victoria Tower Gardens lies at the heart of Westminster, bordered by the Houses of Parliament, the River Thames, Millbank and Lambeth Bridge. The gardens were created during the 1870s by Joseph Bazalgette as part of a project to provide London with a modern sewerage system. Previously, wharves had occupied the site. The gardens, which were extended in 1914, run south from Black Rod Garden and the Houses of Parliament to Lambeth Bridge.

There are a number of interesting features in the gardens. A cast of the sculpture *The Burghers of Calais* by Auguste Rodin, purchased by the British government in 1911, was positioned there in 1915. It is one of the most famous sculptures by Rodin, completed in 1889. Calais commissioned Rodin to create the sculpture in 1884. It tells the story of the year-long siege of Calais in 1347 during the Hundred Years' War. Calais could no longer hold out and surrendered. The English king, Edward III, offered to spare the people of the city if six of its leaders, the Burghers, would surrender themselves to him. Six burghers stepped forward, almost naked, wearing nooses around their necks, and carrying the keys to the city and castle. Fortunately for them, Edward's wife, Queen Philippa, asked that their lives be spared. Their nooses were removed, they were given clothes and dinner and handed money before being escorted out of the camp.

The sculpture in Tower Gardens depicts the burghers holding the keys and wearing the rope halters and shirts of the condemned. Under French law, no more than twelve casts of works of Rodin may be made. Rodin wanted them at ground level to be among the crowd. The controversial sculptor Eric Gill carved the inscription on the pedestal.

The Emmeline and Christabel Pankhurst Memorial commemorates Emmeline and her daughter Christabel, two of the leading British suffragettes. The statue by Arthur George Walker was installed in the Tower Gardens in 1930, two years after Emmeline's death at the age of sixty-nine. Emmeline did not live to see the passing of the Representation of the People Act that extended the vote to all women over the age of twenty-one, a few weeks later.

Emmeline's former bodyguard, Katherine Marshall, began fundraising for a monument to Pankhurst and the unveiling of the statue by former Prime Minister Stanley Baldwin was attended by former suffragettes. In 1958, the statue was moved from its original position in the south of the gardens to a new site further north, and a low stone screen was built flanking the statue. At each end of the screen there are bronze medallions sculpted by Peter Hills, which depict, on the left, the 'prisoner's badge of the Women's Social and Political Union (WSPU) known as the Holloway Brooch, designed by Sylvia Pankhurst in 1909 and on the right is a profile bust of Christabel Pankhurst, who died in 1958.

A notable absence from the commemoration is Sylvia, the daughter of Emmeline Pankhurst and sister of Christabel. Unlike Emmeline and Christabel who dropped the fight for votes for women to support the war effort and supported a limited franchise for upper-class women, Sylvia refused to sacrifice the fight for universal suffrage until it was won. She opposed the First World War and continued her fight against inequality and racism. Emmeline and Christabel eventually expelled her from the Suffragettes. Despite campaigns to have a statue to Sylvia at Westminster, none have materialized. However, a joint campaign by the TUC and City of London Corporation was launched to erect a statue on Clerkenwell Green in Islington in time for the centenary of the Representation of the People Act 1918.

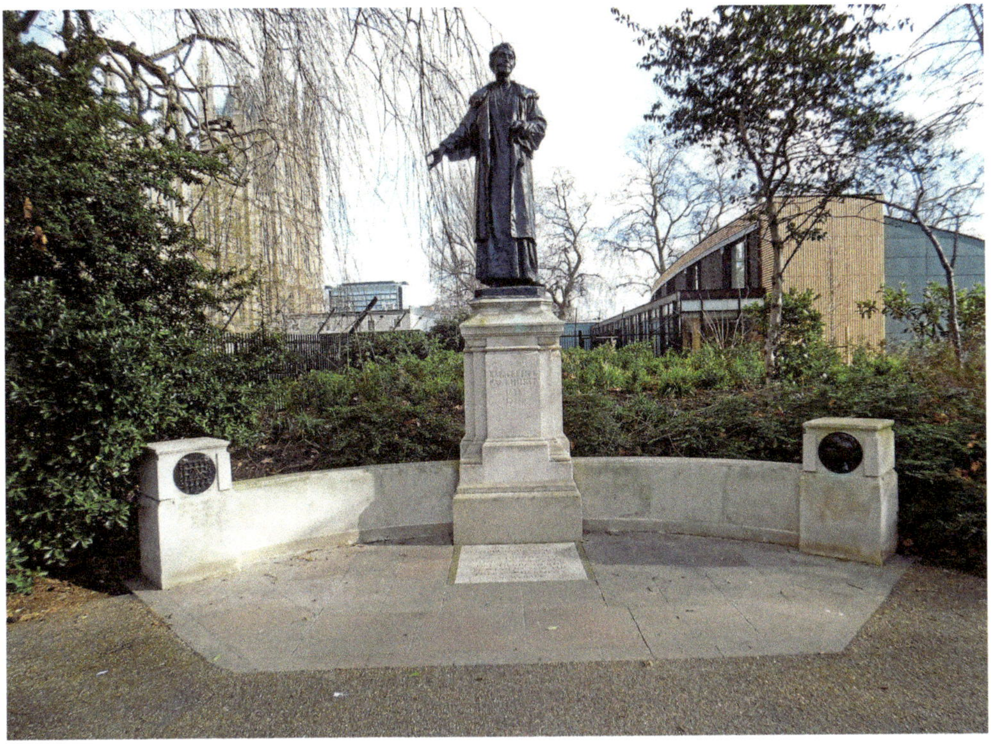

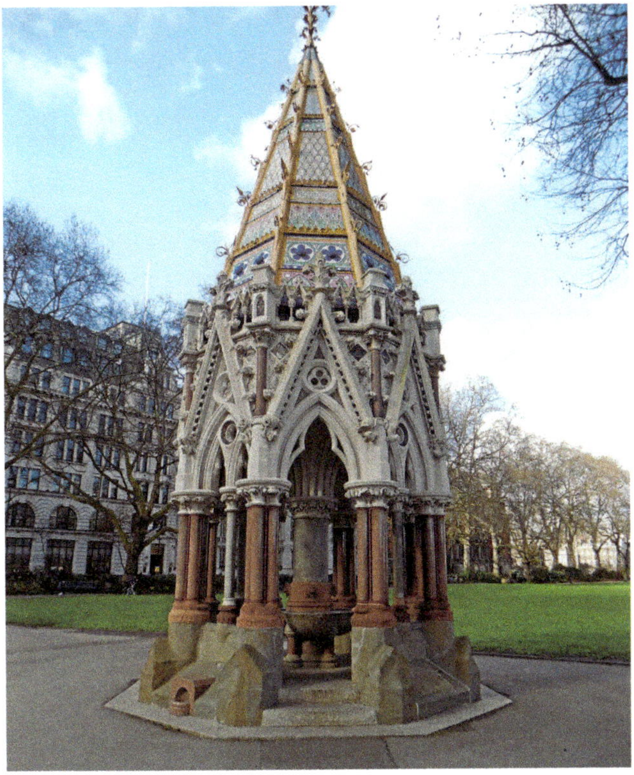

*Above*: The statue of Emmeline Pankhurst with a plaque to Christabel below.

*Right*: Victoria Tower Gardens' Buxton memorial.

The Buxton Memorial Fountain is an elaborate, over-the-top drinking fountain, as well as a memorial to the emancipation of slaves in the British Empire in 1834. It was commissioned and designed by Charles Buxton MP in 1865 and is dedicated to those involved in the abolition movement, including his father Thomas Fowell Buxton and William Wilberforce. The fountain was originally constructed in Parliament Square at a cost of £1,200 but was eventually removed in 1949 and placed in its present position in 1957 in Victoria Tower Gardens. Despite some vandalism, the fountain was restored in 2006–07 as part of the commemoration of the 200th anniversary of the act to abolish the slave trade.

Surmounting the pinnacles at the angles of the octagon are eight figures of bronze, representing the different rulers of England (including the Britons, Romans, Danes, Saxons, Normans and ending with Queen Victoria).

**Nearest tube:** Westminster.

# 29. Vincent Square

Vincent Square is located north of Pimlico Tube Station and south-east of Victoria Station.

Given land values in the centre of London, it is perhaps strange to find a large open space (over 5 hectares) as Vincent Square in such a location. A substantial part of the square is composed of land given over to the outdoor sporting activities of Westminster School.

The square was developed in the eighteenth century on land known as Tothill Fields, which was given over to use as pasture and for the growing of vegetables and herbs. It was also used for various sporting activities and was the frequent location of duels. Under the square lies a very large burial pit containing the remains of victims of the Great Plague of 1665. Its name commemorates Dr William Vincent, a former Dean of Westminster and headmaster of Westminster School.

Vincent Square contains the site of a notorious bear garden. The baiting – some would call it the torture – of bears and bulls was a long-established 'entertainment' involving the setting of specially trained and ferocious dogs on their tethered victims. Baiting was probably at its most popular in the seventeenth century. It enjoyed popularity across the community, attracted huge crowds and bets were laid that saw fortunes lost and won depending on the outcome of the bouts, which were not necessarily one-sided. When baiting was prohibited by law in 1835, it was less for humanitarian reasons than because of a fear that the excited and often drunk crowds might get out of control and destroy property.

Because of its situation, Vincent Square has always been a residential site favoured by politicians, including several prime ministers.

**Nearest tube:** Pimlico, Victoria.

# 30. Waterloo Place

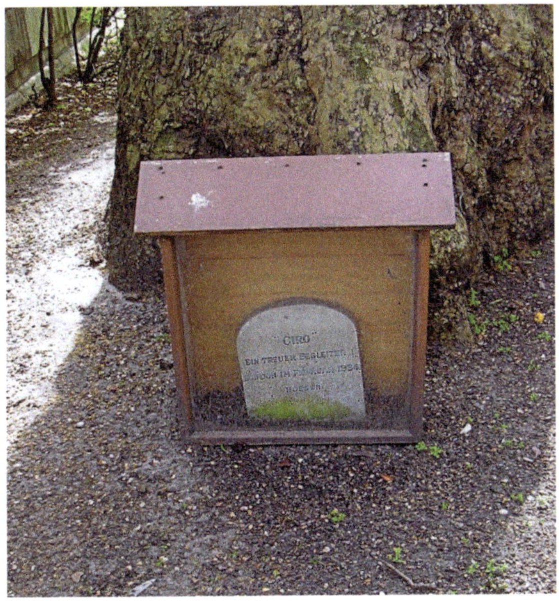

Memorial to Giro, the pet dog of a former German ambassador in Waterloo Place.

It is stretching the definition somewhat if Waterloo Place is going to be described as a square because it is scarcely wider than many of London's streets. It is, however, certainly worthy of more than a second look.

Building work on Waterloo Place commenced in 1816 with the intention that it would, in effect, be a continuation of Regent Street, giving a view that terminated with Carlton House. This much-enlarged mansion, originally erected early in the eighteenth century, was given to Frederick when he was required to live in England by his father, George II, and was made Prince of Wales. There was no love lost between the king and his eldest son. His mother was not fond of him either and refused him permission to come to her as she lay on her deathbed. People viewed Frederick's future role as king with considerable distaste and it was perhaps a relief when he died unexpectedly in 1751. The house continued to be used by royalty and the future George IV, when he himself was Prince of Wales and Prince Regent, held extraordinarily lavish balls and banquets there. He was always very good at spending what, in effect, was money made for him by other people. When George finally became king, he decided that Carlton House was not splendid enough for him in his new role and he had it demolished.

Perhaps the most prominent feature of Waterloo Place is the Duke of York's Column. It has been so often confused with Nelson's Column that a plaque was attached to it to disabuse people of the belief that it was a figure of Nelson on the top. The figure on the top represents someone far less distinguished than Horatio Nelson because it remembers Frederick, Duke of York, the second son of George III who, only because he was the king's

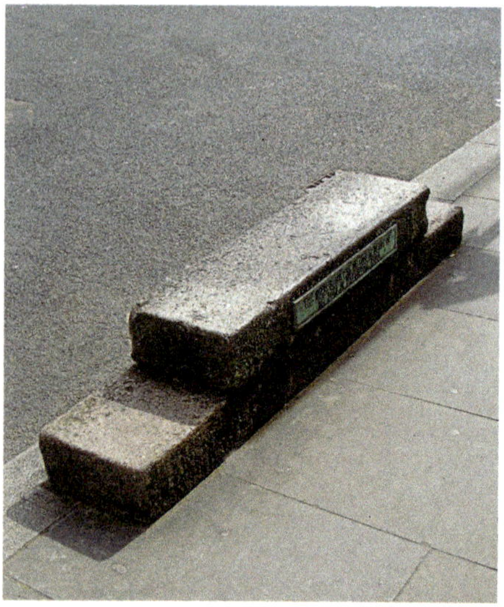

One of the well-known horse mounting blocks installed at the behest of the Duke of Wellington.

son, was made commander-in-chief of the army. He was the 'Grand Old Duke of York', satirised in the famous nursery rhyme. The duke was good at spending money and when he died he had debts that amounted to more than £1.9 million. The money was never recovered and, to add insult to injury, this memorial was erected and paid for by stopping a day's pay from all the men in the army.

Waterloo Place contains something of a cornucopia of statuary. The bronze statue of Captain Robert Falcon Scott (1868–1911) is more poignant than most because it is the handiwork of his wife. Scott was known mainly as an explorer and it is typical of the British to commemorate heroic failure. Scott, of course, was leading a party engaged in a race to the South Pole against another party led by the Norwegian Amundsen. Scott and his party died in the attempt while the Norwegians won and lived to tell the tale.

Six others are immortalised in Waterloo Place. The best known of these is probably Florence Nightingale (1820–1910). She is obviously remembered for her courageous nursing activities during the Crimean War and her pioneering of professional standards for nurses. She was immensely hard-working and focused, but in the Crimea she caught a fever and endured poor health for the rest of her life. She never married but is known to have had many male admirers. She made translations of the writings of Plato and kept sixty cats (not presumably all at the same time). Three of them were named Bismarck, Disraeli and Gladstone. She also had a small owl that she took everywhere in her pocket – it even travelled with her to the Crimea.

Easily overlooked in Waterloo Place are two mounting blocks erected at the request of the Duke of Wellington. A real eccentricity can be found at the top of the steps leading down into The Mall where once stood the German Embassy. There is a gravestone marking the resting place of a dog named Giro. It is considered to be the only Nazi memorial in London although his German owner was not a Nazi at all. Giro was owned by Dr Leopold von Hoesch who was the German Ambassador in London from 1932 to 1936.

**Nearest tubes:** Charing Cross, Piccadilly Circus.

# The Squares of Bloomsbury

Bloomsbury is more or less bounded by Holborn to the south, Euston Road to the north, Tottenham Court Road in the west and Gray's Inn Road to the east. Bloomsbury is associated with the arts, education, and medicine and is home to the British Museum, the Foundling Museum, the Royal Academy of Dramatic Art, at least three notable churches, several hospitals (including Great Ormond Street Hospital for children), the University of London faculties and a number of fashionable squares.

Landowners, notably the Earl of Southampton, the Russell family and the Dukes of Bedford, were responsible for developing Bloomsbury. Although building began in the seventeenth century, the Bloomsbury of today dates largely from the nineteenth century. The streets are typically lined with fashionable Georgian town houses although the southern parts are more institutional and commercial. Bloomsbury has been home to many notable residents and gives its name to the Bloomsbury Group of artists and writers.

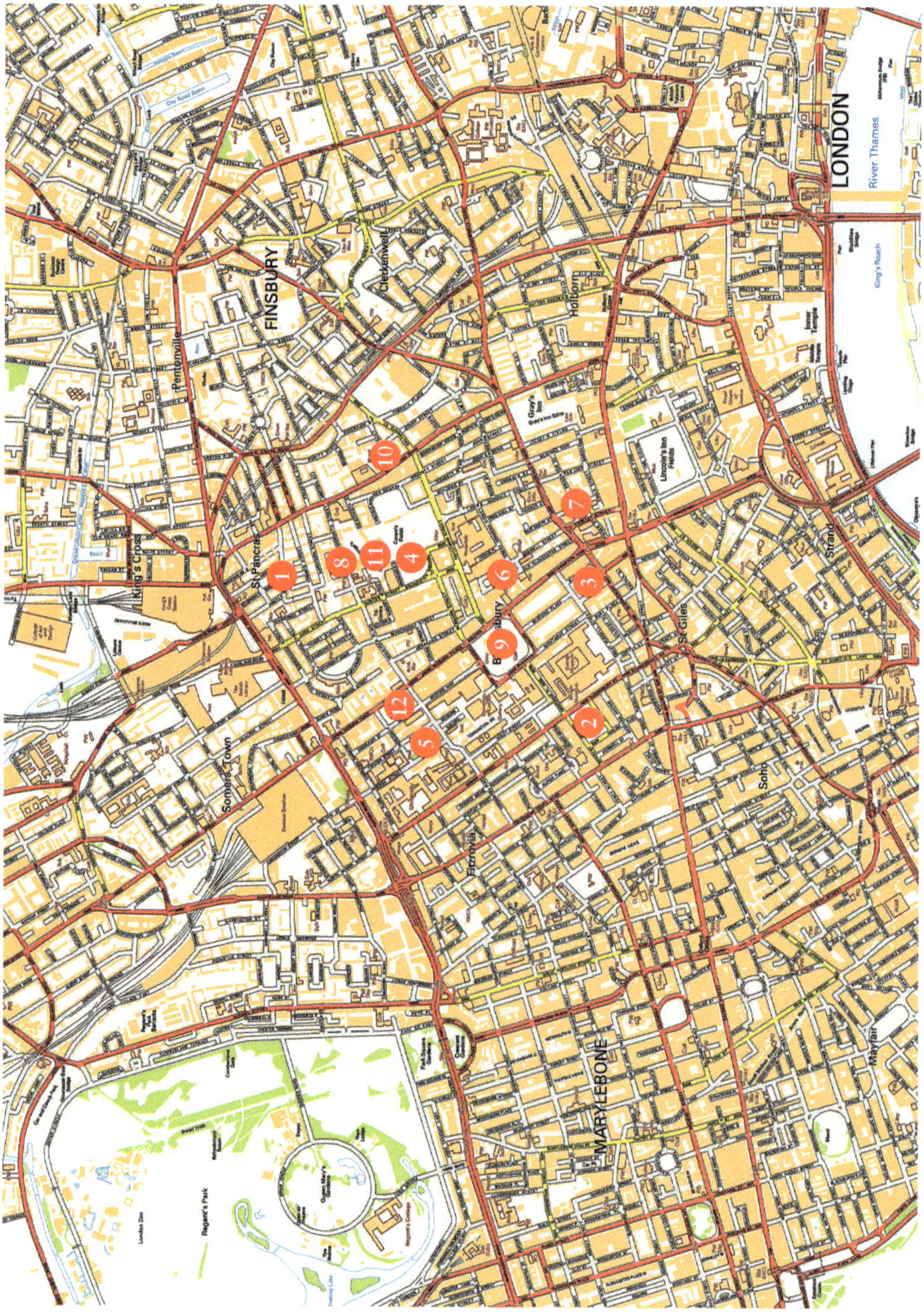
LONDON
River Thames
FINSBURY
Clerkenwell
Holborn
Pentonville
King's Cross
St Pancras
Somers Town
Fitzrovia
St Giles
Strand
Soho
MARYLEBONE
Mayfair
Lincoln's Inn Fields
Regent's Park
1
2
3
4
5
6
7
8
9
10
11
12

# 1. Argyle Square

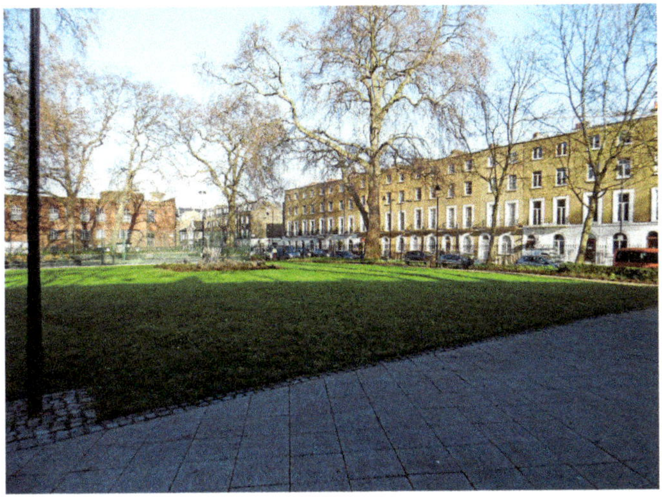

Argyle Square.

Argyle Square lies within a short walking distance south of King's Cross St Pancras Railway Station. The green part of the square is rather basic with few features other than some benches and a play area. The fascinating aspect of this square is its unusual history. Prior to developments in the nineteenth century, the site of Argyle Square was home to the famous Dust Heap, a huge mountain composed of ash and cinders intermingled with rotting vegetable matter, bones and whole animal carcasses. This huge 'black mountain' was teeming with scavengers and is well depicted by Charles Dickens. The great Dust Heap, which was exported to Moscow to produce bricks, was cleared to make way for developments. *The Antiquary* magazine in 1908 stated that the area had several 'huge cinder-hills that formed a small alpine range'. The site was sold in 1826 for £15,000 to the Panarmonion Company. By 1832, Argyle Square was planned but not laid out until the 1840s and named after the Duke of Argyle who owned property nearby.

In 1844, a Swedenborgian New Jerusalem church, which embraced the mystical beliefs of Emanuel Swedenborg, stood on the south side of Argyle Square. However, this was bombed during the Second World War and had to be demolished.

Although Argyle Square was defined in Booth's *Poverty Map* in 1889 as 'comfortable' (having houses with two servants), the surrounding neighbourhood was described as impoverished and 'semi-criminal', typified by brothels and prostitution. Its reputation as one of London's most well-known red-light districts continued well into the late twentieth century when it was subject to a major clean-up in the 1990s. This subsequently gave us the garden square we see today. In 1986, the square became a Women's Peace Camp set up by the King's Cross Women's Committee.

Access to the square was originally restricted to the residents but it is now a public garden. The square, which is enclosed by reproduction cast-iron railings, contains six mature London plane trees from the earlier layout and is surrounded by formal terraces of elegant architecture. The Georgian buildings include original iron railings around basement light wells, decorative balustrades and first-floor balconies.

**Nearest tube:** King's Cross St Pancras.

## 2. Bedford Square

Bedford Square is situated to the south-east of Goodge Street Tube Station. The Earls of Bedford, later elevated to Dukes, had their main London landholdings in Covent Garden and Bloomsbury. To this day, many of the streets recall family names such as Russell or places on their provincial estates.

Bedford Square is notable for being the only remaining complete Georgian square in the Bloomsbury district. It was built between 1775 and 1780 and was highly fashionable in its early years. The square's social exclusivity was emphasised by gates and attendant flunkeys who were instructed to exclude all but residents and those who could prove that they had legitimate business in the square. Even then, only the heads or senior partners of those with clients or customers residing in the square would be admitted. The gates to the square were removed in the early 1890s but the gardens have remained private. In their original form and design, the gardens acted as a model for many later squares. They have frequently been used as the location for films.

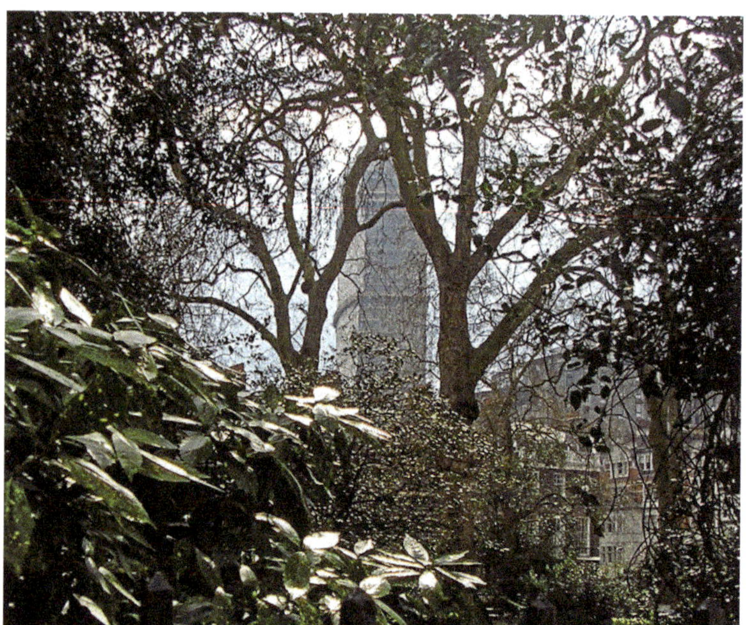

Bedford Square with a view of Centre Point from the square's gardens.

Henry Cavendish lived at No. 11 from 1796 until his death in 1810. He was one of the greatest scientists in British history but one of the least known because of his excessively reclusive nature. He was born in 1731 into a branch of the Cavendish Family, the head of which was the fabulously rich Duke of Devonshire. In 1783, he inherited his father's estate and, soon after, a large legacy from an aunt and he became an immensely rich man.

Cavendish was the first to identify the element hydrogen, was the first to realise that water was a compound of hydrogen and oxygen, and he did pioneering work with electrical resistance and used measurements of gravity to calculate the mean density of Planet Earth – which were extraordinarily close to later figures produced by much more sophisticated means. He was often uncomfortable in company and could not handle relations with servants. He could not bear to meet them face-to-face and ordered dinner, which always included mutton, by leaving messages on the hall table. His lifestyle was extremely frugal and he did little to publicise his pioneering research, but kept copious notebooks which, after his death, showed the full extent and value of his work.

The highly unpopular Lord Eldon (1751–1838), when Chancellor, moved into No. 6 in 1802 and lived there until around 1819. In 1815, during riots – a common phenomenon in London – angry rioters smashed the windows and then broke in, hoping to lynch Eldon. Fortunately for him, he was not in at the time. As Attorney General, he had made enemies by suspending habeas corpus from 1794 to 1801. This was part of his zealous persecution of 'subversive' elements. Anyone campaigning for greater social justice was subversive according to Eldon. He was also hated for opposing Catholic emancipation, for his opposition to the abolition of slavery, for his hostility to ending imprisonment for debt and his unremitting aversion to the slightest widening of the vote or any other progressive political reform. Former Prime Minister H. H. Asquith was also a previous resident of the square.

Many of the Bloomsbury squares were destroyed or partially ruined after the First World War. Bedford Square remained reasonably intact, preserving much of its original late eighteenth-century character. During the Second World War, the Georgian iron railings of the Bloomsbury squares were claimed as part of the official campaign for 'goodwill' scrap metal. However, the 'beautiful railings' at Bedford Square were reprieved partly as a result of the defiance of the 12th Duke of Bedford (who was a pacifist) and the efforts of the Georgian Group.

**Nearest tube:** Russell Square, Holborn, Goodge Street, Tottenham Court Road.

## 3. Bloomsbury Square

Bloomsbury Square was the first place in London to be called a square. It is a short walk from Holborn Underground Station. Turn west along New Oxford Street then north onto Southampton Place to find it.

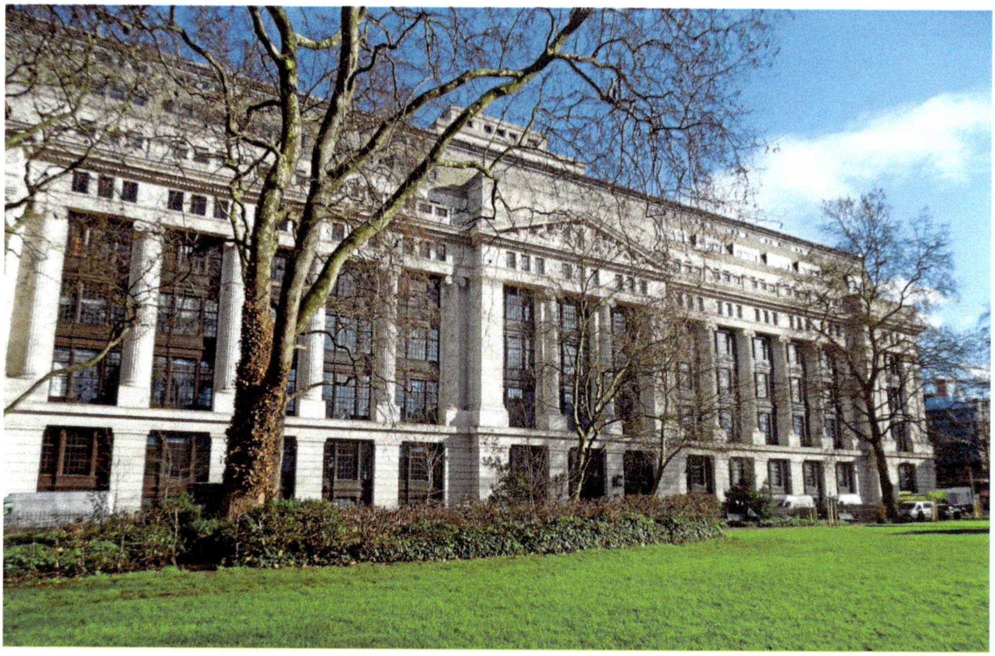

The imposing Victoria House in Bloomsbury Square.

In 1665, the diarist John Evelyn recorded that he dined with the Lord Treasurer, the Earl of Southampton, in Bloomsbury, 'where he [Southampton] was building a noble square or piazza, a little towne'. The 'little towne' was a reference to the fact that Bloomsbury had become one of the most sought-after suburbs in London. In 1669, the Earl's daughter, Rachel, married into the Russell family, the Dukes of Bedford, and the square was renamed Bloomsbury Square.

In April 1694, an infamous duel took place in the square. Twenty-three-year-old John Law, a Scottish economist, fought Edward 'Beau' Wilson (who had challenged Law over the affections of Elizabeth Villiers), killing him with a single thrust of his sword. Law was charged with murder and sentenced to death, but he eventually escaped and went on to become France's Controller General of Finances. However, he contributed to bringing about a severe financial crisis in France that impacted right across Europe. Law fled France, ending his days in Venice in 1729.

In 1806, an Act allowed the Duke of Bedford to construct 'any statue, column or ornamental erection but no other building in the Square'. At the northern end of the gardens is a bronze statue of Charles James Fox (1749–1806) by Sir Richard Westmacott, erected in 1816. Fox was a leading radical, a member of the Whig party and an associate of the Bedford family.

Fox was famed for his womanising, drinking and gambling. He was twice bankrupted and had to rely on his father to pay off £120,000 of his gambling debts. He once claimed that he gambled from Tuesday night until Friday night without sleep and only took time off to debate in the House of Commons. Fox had great charm and was a powerful orator. He held a firm belief that power should flow from the people, a desire for wide-ranging reform, a strong preference for peace rather than war and he supported the anti-slavery movement. His statue was restored in 2006 to commemorate the bicentenary of Fox's death and was unveiled by Michael Foot.

The layout to the gardens changed by the early twentieth century. There were scattered trees on the lawn, oval shrubberies at each corner and a central shrubbery. The gardens remained private up until the Second World War when the railings were removed and

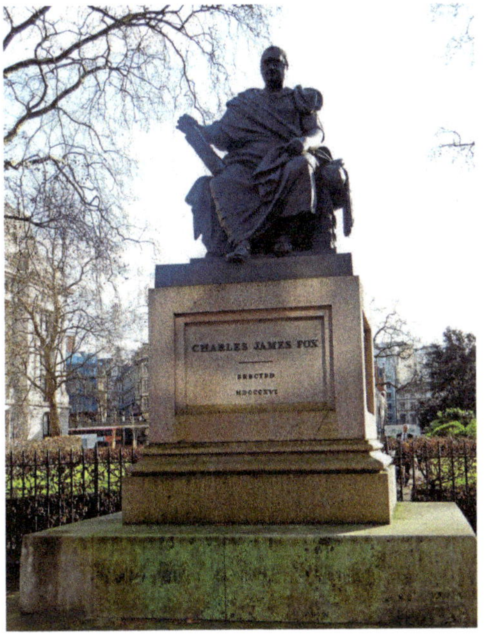


The statue of Charles James Fox in Bloomsbury Square Gardens.

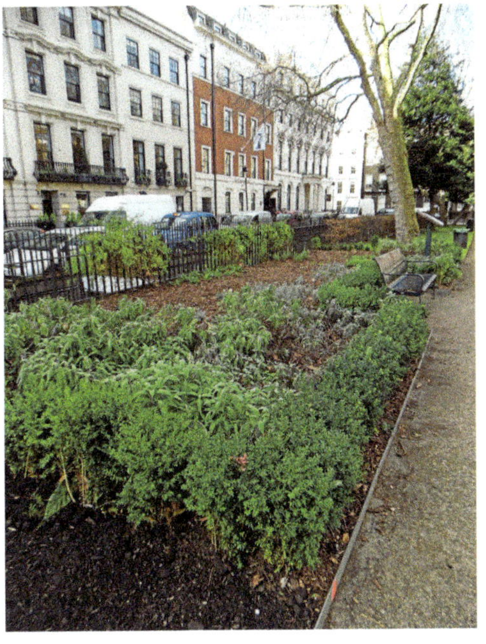

Physic Garden, Bloomsbury Square Gardens.

melted down for armaments. This allowed other people to come into the gardens for the first time and, in 1950, it was officially made public. Between 1971 and 1973, further alterations in the south of the square took place when a car park was built underneath.

The square increasingly attracted middle-class professionals. Edwin Lutyens (1869–1944), an Architect of the Arts and Crafts movement, lived here in the early twentieth century. Lutyens designed many buildings and monuments including the Cenotaph in Whitehall. Across to the west, is White Hall, where dermatologist Dr Robert Willan (1757–1812) lived. Willan was the first person to classify diseases of the skin. Former Prime Minister Benjamin Disraeli (1804–81) lived at No. 6 between 1817 and 1824.

On the east side of the square was the home of Lord Chief Justice William Mansfield (1705–93), once No. 29, which was burned down in June 1780 during the anti-Catholic Gordon Riots. A section of the mob went to the square and at least four men and a woman were killed and several more rioters injured. The square was cleared but the mob returned with tar-soaked rope to burn down Lord Mansfield's house. Mansfield managed to escape through the back of the house onto what is now Southampton Row. Three of the rioters who attacked the house, John Gray, Charles Kent and Letitia Holland, were executed on Saturday 20 June in the north-east part of Bloomsbury Square as it was the practice for some criminals to be hanged as close to the scene of their crime as possible.

Beneath the gallows, Gray leaned heavily on a crutch, owing to the injuries he had sustained during the riots, while Kent teetered on his wooden leg and turned 'so pale he looked like a ghost'. Both men prayed with great 'fervency' before the cart moved away, leaving them suspended. Charles Dickens's novel describes the attack on Mansfield's mansion:

> The mob gathering round Lord Mansfield's house, had called on those within to open the door, and receiving no reply forced an entrance ... they then began to demolish the house with great fury, and setting fire to it ... [which] involved in a common ruin the whole of the costly furniture, the plate and jewels, a beautiful gallery of pictures, the rarest collection of manuscripts ever possessed ... [and] the great Law Library.
>
> *Barnaby Rudge* (1841)

The character of the eponymous Barnaby Rudge features as one of those arrested and sentenced to hang on a scaffold erected in Bloomsbury Square but he is reprieved at the last minute.

The east side of the square is dominated by the impressive Grade II-listed neoclassical building called Victoria House, constructed in the 1920s. The building was extensively renovated in 2003.

Sir Hans Sloane (1660–1753) physician, collector and benefactor of the British Museum lived, along with his collection of curiosities and books, at No. 3 Bloomsbury Place. So large was his collection, he also purchased No. 4. After his death, the British government used his collection as the foundation for the British Museum. In honour of Sloane, children from Eleanor Palmer Primary School in Camden designed and planted a physic garden in the gardens in 2012. The project was supported by the Heritage Lottery Fund.

**Nearest tube:** Holborn.

# 4. Brunswick Square

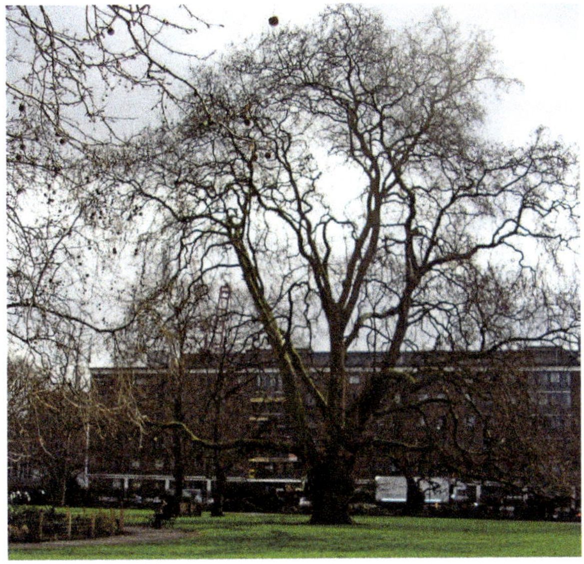

Some experts believe that the tree in Brunswick Square Gardens is the oldest plane tree in London.

Brunswick Square is north-east of Russell Square Tube Station. The square was built between 1795 and 1802. None of the original buildings survive.

It is named after Caroline of Brunswick-Wolfenbuttel, wife of the Prince Regent, later George IV. George was always a profligate spender, which meant that he frequently had a cash-flow problem. A marriage was engineered for him and Caroline. It was a lifeline for George because of Caroline's immense wealth which legally became his at matrimony. The negotiations were completed before the two had actually seen each other. When they met for the first time, it was a case of instant mutual antipathy. The wedding had to go ahead but George spent the first night of matrimony totally incapacitated by drink. However, the marriage was clearly consummated when, in 1796, their only child was born. George promptly left Caroline, who took herself off to Europe. She returned to England in 1820 when George succeeded to the throne, demanding what she regarded as her rights as Queen. Her consistently outrageous behaviour endeared her to the London crowd, if only because George was no model of propriety himself. Caroline's death in 1821 prevented further embarrassment.

Prominent members of the 'Bloomsbury Set' including Virginia Woolf and John Maynard Keynes lived at No.38.

In 1739, George II granted Thomas Coram (1668–1751) a charter to establish 'A Hospital for the maintenance and Education of Exposed and Deserted Children'. Thomas Coram was a native of Dorset who settled in London in 1719 after travelling abroad extensively. He had become concerned about the large numbers of ragged and seemingly homeless infants he saw on London's streets, particularly in the poorer districts. Many of them were illegitimate and abandoned by their mothers, partly because of their poverty and the stigma attached to the mothers of children born out of wedlock and to the children themselves. The resulting 'hospital' was built on land formerly known as Lamb's Conduit Fields. Later, the impecunious governors sold some of the land that became Brunswick Square. This is open to the public in daylight hours and contains a plane tree reckoned to be one of the oldest in London.

Coram is commemorated with a statue outside No. 40, which is the Foundling Museum. This has exhibits associated with Coram in addition to much material associated with the artist William Hogarth and the composer Handel, both of whom were supporters of the hospital. The relatively little-known Foundling Hospital could be said to be Britain's first children's charity and its first public art gallery. Running along the west side of the Square is the controversial brutalist architecture of Brunswick Centre.

**Nearest tube:** King's Cross St Pancras, Russell Square.

## 5. Gordon Square

Gordon Square is south of Euston Road along Gordon Street. It is a large square and is popular with people who work nearby as well as students from the University of London.

The square was named after the 6th Duke of Bedford's wife, Lady Georgiana Gordon. It was begun by master builder Thomas Cubitt (1788–1855) as one of a pair with nearby Tavistock Square in the 1820s and was completed forty years later. It was originally for the private use of the residents of the surrounding houses although it has long been a public square. In 1920, the Duke of Bedford agreed to sell the site to the government for the building of the University of London.

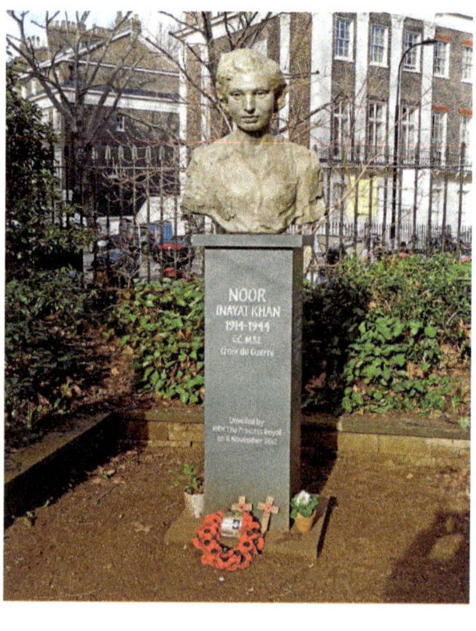


The bust of SOE agent Noor Inayat Khan in Gordon Square Gardens.

The gardens have a variety of shrubs as well as many mature London plane trees. In the south-west corner is a section of woodland ground flora that includes bluebells, cow parsley and dog violets. Two commemorative statues have been installed in the garden in recent years: a sculpture (by Shenda Amery) of the Indian poet, philosopher and Nobel Laureate Rabindranath Tagore (1861–1941), in 2011, and a memorial bust of Noor Inayat Khan (1914–1944) unveiled in 2012. Noor, who had once lived nearby, was a Special Operations Executive (SOE) agent who infiltrated occupied France. She was executed at Dachau concentration camp and was honoured with the GC, MBE and Croix de Guerre.

On the west side of Gordon Square is the Grade I-listed Church of Christ the King, built between 1851 and 1854 for the Catholic Apostolic Church, a group who believed in the imminent Second Coming of Christ. However, over the years, it has had a number of different functions – by 2005, it had become the headquarters of Forward in Faith, an Anglican movement founded in 1992 who were opposed to the ordination of women.

Dr Williams's library stands to the west side of Gordon Square. The library was founded using the estate of Dr Daniel Williams (1643–1716) as a theological library. The library opened in 1729 at Red Cross Street and moved frequently until the acquisition of its present home in Gordon Square in 1890. In July 2006, the library offered for sale at Sotheby's its copy of Shakespeare's *First Folio*. The book sold for £2.8 million.

On the east side of the square, at No. 46, lived Sir Leslie Stephen, first editor of the *National Dictionary of Biography*. Stephen died in 1904 and the house was then occupied by his daughter, Virginia, later Woolf, (1882–1941) and her siblings. It was here, and in subsequent houses in Bloomsbury, that the Bloomsbury Group – made up of writers, intellectuals and artists – was established. Famous members included John Maynard Keynes, Vanessa Bell, E. M. Forster, Roger Fry and writer Lytton Strachey. Strachey lived at No. 51 Gordon Square, allegedly in a ménage à trois with painter Dora Carrington and her husband Ralph Partridge.

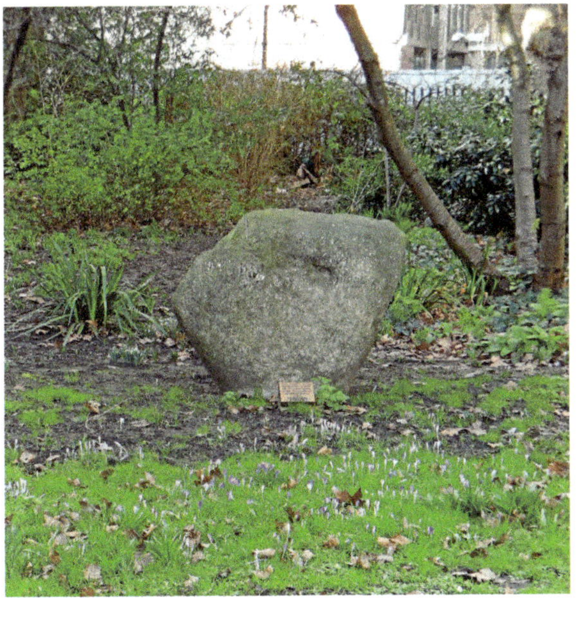

'Sarsen Stone', Gordon Square Gardens.

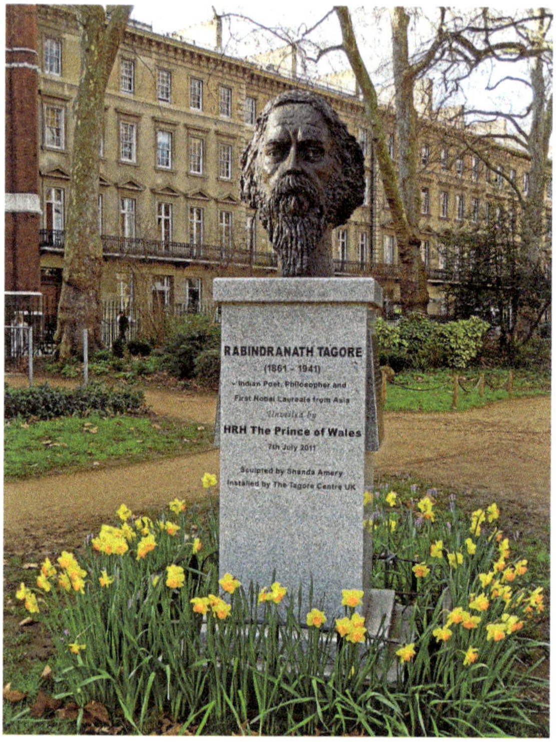


Bust of Indian poet, philosopher and Nobel Laureate Rabindranath Tagore.

At the northern end of the gardens stands a large stone. It is in commemoration of the University College London Institute of Archaeology (which is to the north of the square) to celebrate seventy-five years of its role in leading global archaeology. The sarsen stone was donated by a farmer in the Avebury area of Wiltshire and is recognisable as an archaeological icon due to their presence at sites such as Stonehenge.

In 1916, No. 46 Gordon Square was bought by economist and fellow Bloomsbury Group member John Maynard Keynes (1883–1946) and remained his London home for thirty years. Keynes was one of the century's most influential economists and was instrumental in monetary negotiations with the United States. If his public life was busy, exhausting or exhilarating, then he applied the same sort of unconventional adventurism to his personal life. Keynes collected and catalogued his sexual activities by keeping detailed records of encounters, with names or initials of partners. His early sexual relationships were exclusively with men but he married Lydia Lopokova, a well-known Russian ballerina in 1925. In the early years of their relationship, Keynes maintained an affair with a younger man, Sebastian Sprott, in tandem with Lopokova.

The surgeon Sir Frederick Treves (1853–1923) lived at No. 18 between 1880 and 1885. He held appointments at the London Hospital and made a special study of the abdomen and first gave appendicitis its name. His successful operation on Edward VII gave him worldwide fame. However, his fame today is more often associated with his friendship with Joseph Merrick, the 'Elephant Man'.

**Nearest tube:** Russell Square.

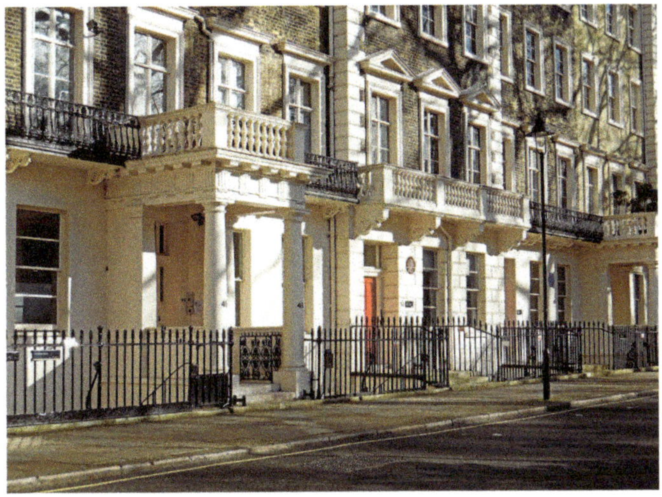

Gordon Square terraced houses.

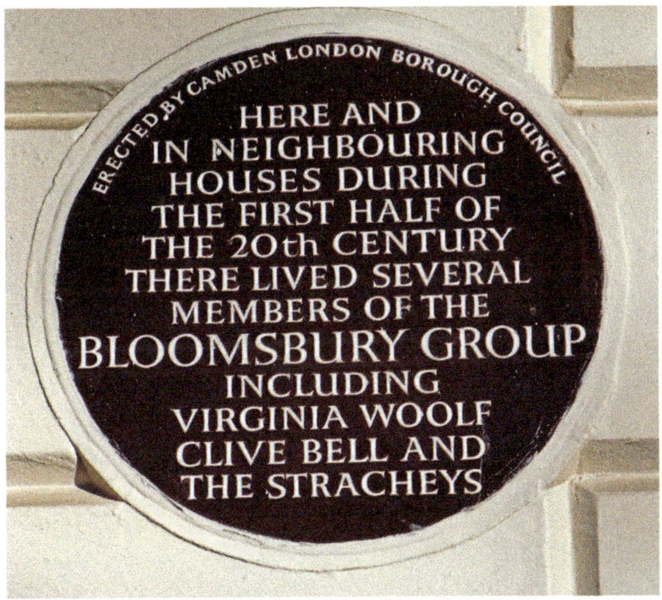


A plaque to the Bloomsbury Group.

## 6. Queen Square

Queen Square is a short walk south of Russell Square Tube Station. The square was built around 1713–25 and was named after Queen Anne. All the original buildings have gone. At one time it housed a reservoir supplying the site of the Greyfriars to the east in Newgate Street. This monastery had been established in the thirteenth century. At the south end of the square, there is an iron pump which acts as a reminder of its earlier usage.

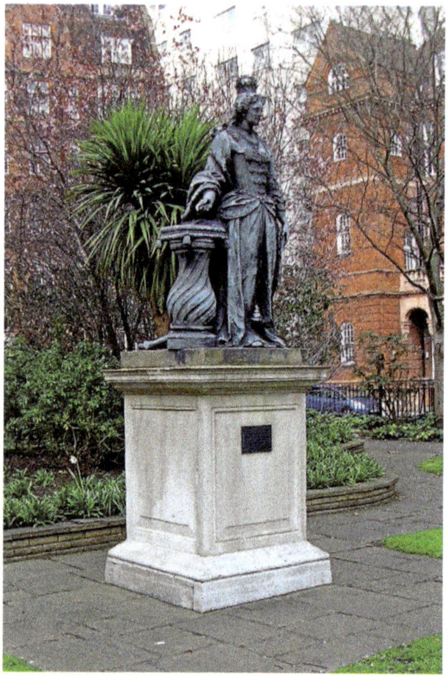

A statue of Queen Charlotte, the long-suffering wife of King George III, in Queen Square.

In the gardens, which are public, there is a lead statue of Queen Charlotte (1744–1818) from around 1775. She was the wife of George III and her full name was Sophia Charlotte of Mecklenburg-Strelitz. She supported her husband through his various travails and also engaged in charitable and other good works when she wasn't having one of her fifteen children. There is a plaque with verses by Ted Hughes and Philip Larkin that commemorates the lucky escape of around 1,000 people who escaped without injury when a Zeppelin came down and exploded in 1915. This was unveiled in 1997. A cast-iron water pump dated 1840 stands to the south of the square and there is a small waste-water trough surrounded by Gothic-style bollards.

A sculpture commissioned by the friends of Great Ormond Street was erected in 2001. This reflects the fact that the square and its immediate neighbourhood had a substantial presence of hospitals and other medical care.

Another sculpture of 1997 depicts a cat called Sam about to jump off a wall onto the ground. This commemorates a local resident, cat lover and nurse Patricia (Penny) Penn (1914–92). Described as a 'formidable lady' – but very popular – she had been very active in the area in the 1970s, campaigning to protect it from developers and to preserve historic buildings.

An early resident of what was then the highly fashionable square was Dr Charles Burney and his daughter Fanny. In 1771–72, the square was still open at its northern end and Fanny, who kept a fascinating diary, describes her delight in being able to look northwards to the green rural delights of the high ground around Hampstead and Highgate.

On the eastern side of the square there was once an academy for genteel young ladies. When they attended services at the nearby church of St George the Martyr, they travelled in a coach despite the church being so close by. This was so that they could practise climbing into and out of the coach in the decorous fashion expected of well-bred young ladies. This ability was clearly considered to be of vital importance because when the coach was no longer roadworthy, it was kept under cover and it was still used for practise in the honing of these essential social skills.

On the west side of the square is the uniquely named Queen's Larder pub. The building owes this curious name to reputedly having once housed a store of food which was used by Queen Charlotte to feed her husband George III during those times when he was receiving treatment in premises nearby.

**Nearest tube:** Russell Square, Holborn.

# 7. Red Lion Square

Red Lion Square lies on the boundary of Bloomsbury and Holborn and is a short walk north-east of Holborn Station. Originally Red Lion Fields, this small but interesting square was laid out in 1684 by Nicholas Barbon. The 'Red Lyon' Inn was the most important hostelry in Holborn, so much so that Red Lion Street and the adjoining square were named after it.

Red Lion Square was fashionable in the early eighteenth century but had become decidedly unfashionable by the mid-nineteenth century. Part of the square's historical fame rests upon the well-documented, but questionable, story regarding Oliver Cromwell's

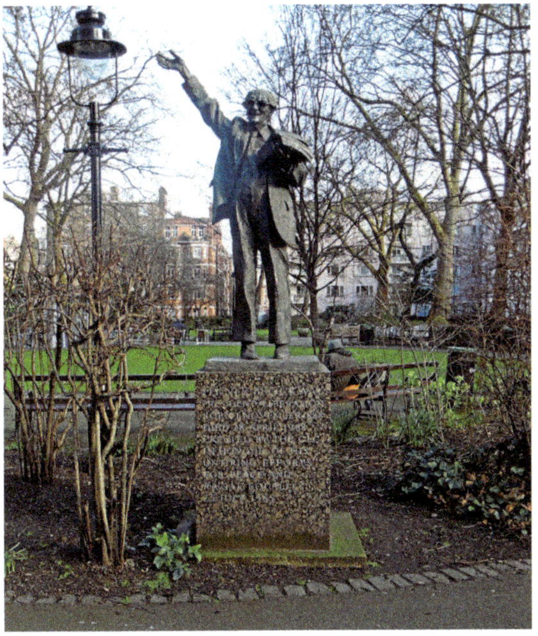

The statue of Fenner Brockway, anti-war activist and politician, Red Lion Square Gardens.

body and his subsequent haunting of the square. It was reputed that the bodies of the regicides – Oliver Cromwell, his son-in-law Henry Ireton and the judge John Bradshaw (who was judge at the trial of Charles I) – were kept at Red Lion Square before being ritually 'executed' at Tyburn the following day.

Why they were taken to Red Lion Square is something of a mystery. Cromwell had died in 1658 and had originally been buried in Westminster Abbey; Ireton had died earlier in 1651 and Bradshaw more recently in 1659. Following the Restoration of the Monarchy in 1660, the new parliament ordered the bodies of Cromwell, Bradshaw and Ireton to be disinterred, posthumously tried and executed at Tyburn where they were gibbetted and beheaded before being buried in a pit by the gallows. The heads were then displayed from the roof of Westminster Hall. The story is further cloaked in mystery by reference to an obelisk that stood in the square in the eighteenth century but had gone by the 1790s. The obelisk was rumoured to have served as a dedication to the bones of Cromwell, Ireton and Bradshaw that were said to lie beneath. It's a highly unlikely tale, but many historic rumours gain such mythical status.

In the 1680s, property speculator Nicholas Barbon (1640–98) saw the possibilities of developing Red Lion Square for a new housing project. His full name was Nicholas If-Jesus-Christ-Had-Not-Died-For-Thee-Thou-Hadst-Been-Damned Barebone – Puritan families often burdened their offspring with religious slogans. There were objections to the development from the lawyers of nearby Gray's Inn. Nonetheless, they lost the case but refused to give in and a pitched battle broke out in the square between the workmen and around 100 lawyers armed with bricks and other sundry building materials. The 'battle' resulted in many on both sides being injured.

Notable residents of the square include William Morris, Dante Gabriel Rossetti (one of the founders of the Pre-Raphaelite school of painting) and Edward Burne-Jones. A house in the north-west corner bears a plaque to these artists. John Harrison, a brilliant carpenter-turned-clockmaker, was the world-renowned inventor of the marine chronometer, a long-sought-after device for solving the problem of establishing the East–West position or longitude of a ship at sea. He lived at No. 12, where he died in 1776. There is a blue plaque dedicated to him on the corner of Summit House.

The square was badly damaged by bombing during the Second World War, hence only a few of the original houses still survive. Nos 14–17 were built around 1686 but were given a new façade in the nineteenth century. At the western entrance of the garden is a statue to anti-war activist Fenner Brockway, installed in 1986. Brockway attended the unveiling but died two years later. There is also a bust of philosopher Bertrand Russell. It is appropriate that the gardens contain these memorials to two notable humanists. Conway Hall, home of the South Place Ethical Society (thought to be the oldest surviving free-thought organisation in the world) and the National Secular Society opens on to the square.

The Red Lion disorders took place on the 15 June 1974 when a meeting by the extreme right wing National Front was held in Conway Hall. This resulted in a protest by anti-fascist groups. Confrontation between the groups became inevitable and around forty policemen were treated for injuries as well as many demonstrators with around fifty arrested. Amid the fighting, the body of one of the demonstrators, Kevin Gately, a mathematics student at the University of Warwick, was found on the ground. An inquest concluded that Kevin had

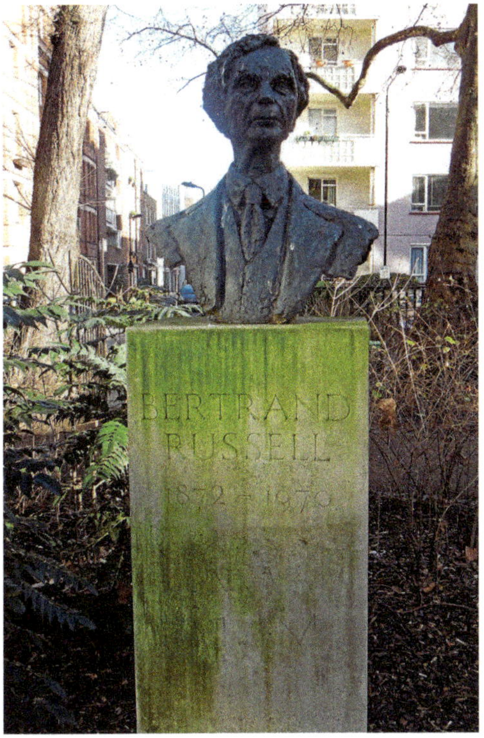


*Right*: The bust of Bertrand Russell, philosopher, in Red Lion Square Gardens.

*Below*: A plaque to artists Rossetti, Morris and Burne-Jones.

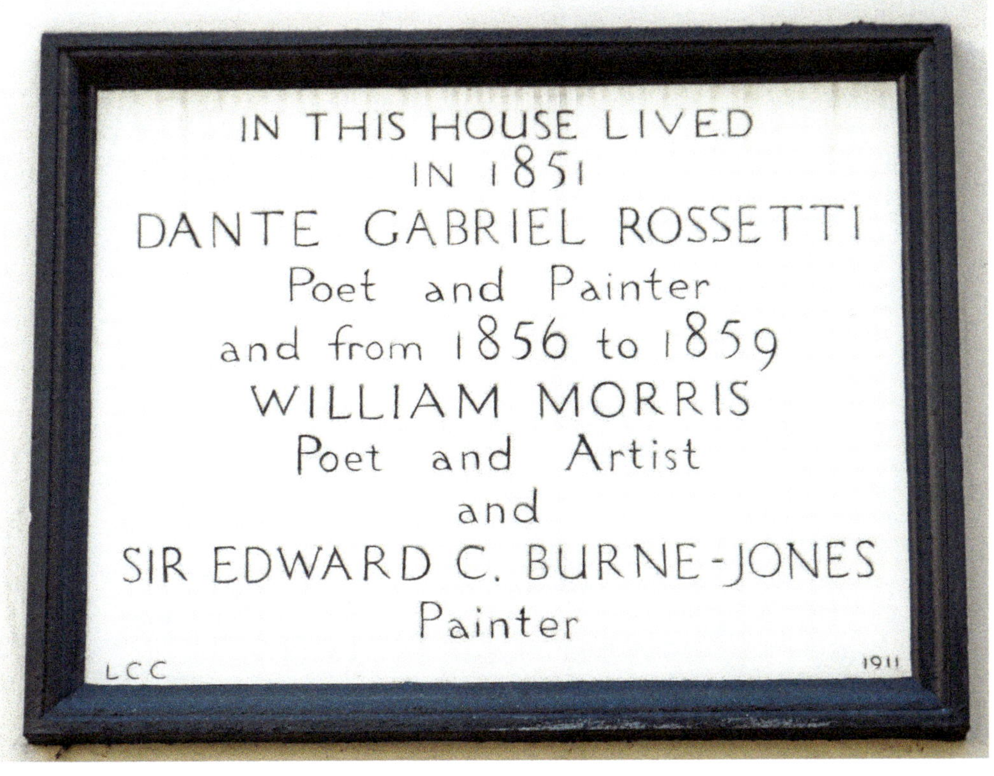

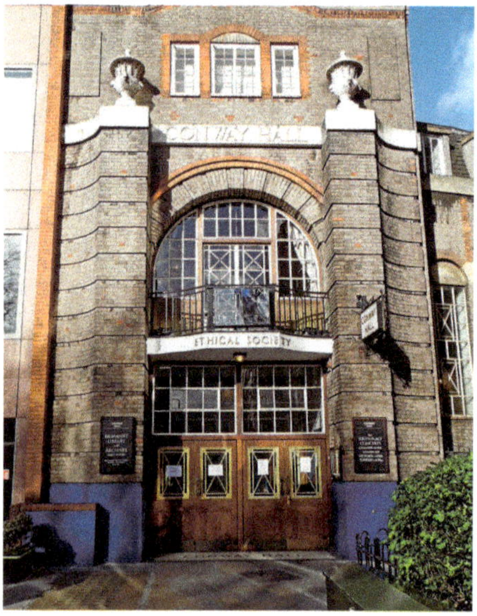

Conway Hall, Red Lion Square.

died from a brain haemorrhage from a blow by a blunt instrument. He had the unfortunate distinction of being the first person to die in a public demonstration in Britain since 1919.

The square is also home to the Royal College of Anaesthetists and the College of Emergency Medicine.

**Nearest tube:** Holborn.

# 8. Regent Square Gardens

Regent Square Gardens is located south of King's Cross St Pancras Tube Station near to St George's Gardens. The square was built around 1820 and the Regency terraces survive only on the south side. A Gothic church stood on the south side but was bombed in the Second World War and replaced by the United Reform Church. The gardens were originally built from 1829 for the use of residents in the surrounding houses but later opened to the public.

Changes took place to the gardens from the 1970s and the current layout dates from 1995 as a result of improvements around King's Cross. Among the features are six mature plane trees, several metal benches along the paths and a few modern lamp posts.

A K2 telephone box of 1927 is located on the south-west side. William Hartnell (the first Doctor Who) can be counted as one the square's former residents as well as the English realist artist Sir William Coldstream (1908–97).

**Nearest tube:** King's Cross St Pancras.

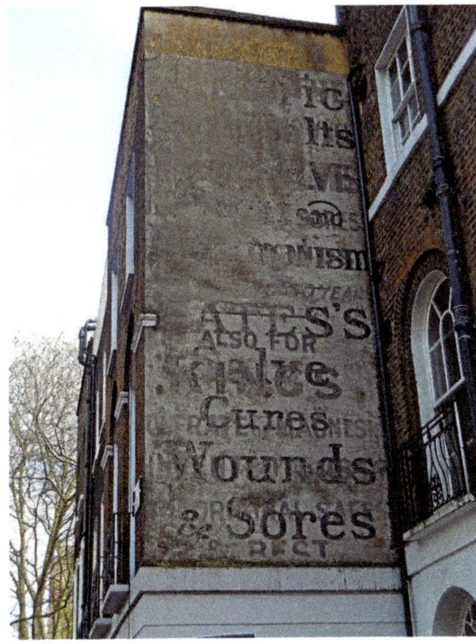


A ghost sign in Regent Square.

# 9. Russell Square

Russell Square is a short walk to the west of Russell Square Station and is one of London's largest squares. It was laid out in 1800 and named after the surname of the landlords, the Dukes of Bedford, as are other local street names such as Bedford Square, Bedford Place, Bedford Avenue, Bedford Row and Bedford Way. The statue on the south side of the square is that of Francis Russell, the 5th Duke of Bedford (1765–1802) who was responsible for much of the development of Central Bloomsbury, including the square itself.

The houses of Russell Square were popular among those in the legal profession. The great law reformer Sir Samuel Romilly (1757–1818), who repealed many capital offences, committed suicide by cutting his throat at No. 21 after the death of his wife. In his book *Vanity Fair* (1848), William Makepeace Thackeray suggests that Russell Square was the home of vulgar upstarts and newly rich merchants.

Adjacent to the square's gardens are large terraced houses with a number of the original houses still surviving, notably on the southern and western sides. The west side of the square is dominated by the University of London Senate House, while on the east side is the imposing late nineteenth-century Hotel Russell.

Set into the pavement on the east side of Russell Square (near the junction with Guilford Street) is a sign pointing to the Turkish Baths. The baths were built in 1913 as part of an extension to the Imperial Hotel. They were demolished with the rest of the hotel in 1966. The statues, which adorned part of the baths, were rescued and now sit in the courtyard of the new Imperial Hotel.

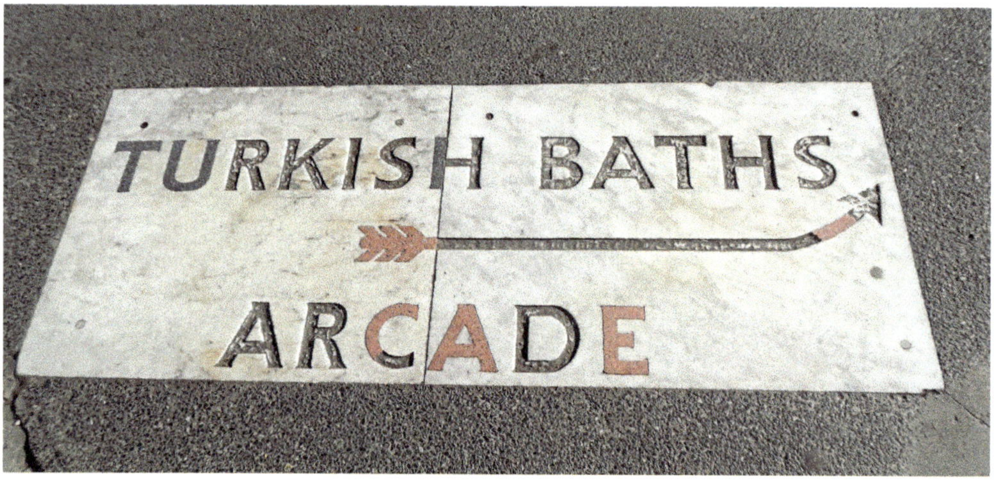


The sign on the pavement to the Turkish Baths, Russell Square.

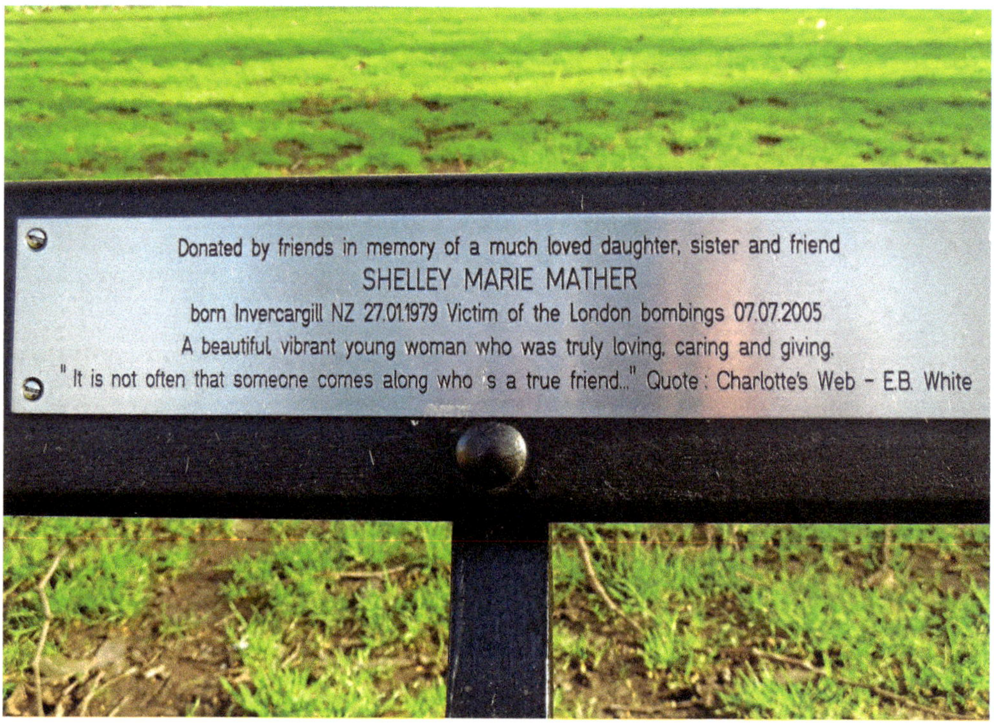


A dedication to a 7/7 victim in Russell Square.

At Nos 23–24 Bloomsbury Square is a plaque that reads, 'T. S. Eliot, poet and publisher, worked here for Faber & Faber, 1925–1965'.

In the gardens, a memorial plaque and a young oak tree commemorate the fifty-two victims killed in the bombings of 7 July 2005. One of the bombings took place on an Underground train from King's Cross to Russell Square Tube Station and another occurred

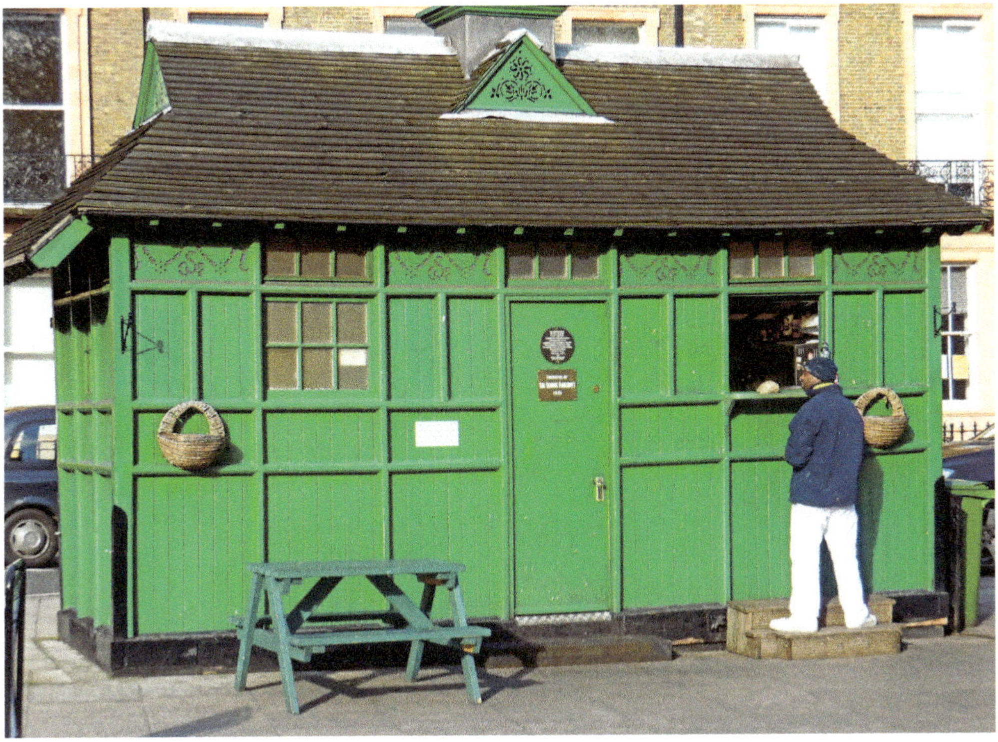

*Above*: A cabman's shelter, Russell Square.

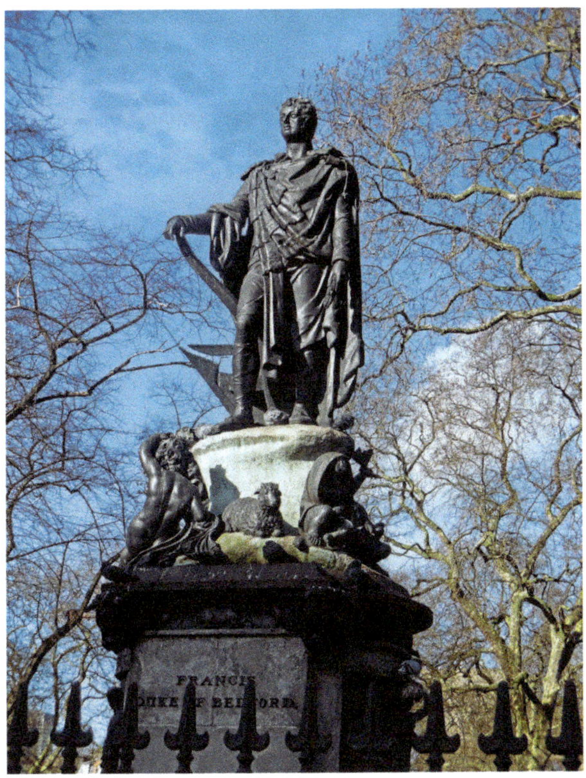


*Right*: The statue of the Duke of Bedford in Russell Square.

on a bus at Tavistock Square, near Russell Square. An inscription on one of the benches is to twenty-six-year-old Shelley Marie Mather, a victim of the bombings.

The square's large and attractive public garden was restored and replanted in 2002 along with the installation of a fountain. On the west side of Russell Square stands a cabman's shelter, a Grade II-listed building. Over sixty of these shelters were built between 1875 and 1914 with a special fund set up by Lord Shaftesbury and the support of other philanthropists. Many of these shelters were staffed by an attendant who sold food and (non-alcoholic) drink to the cabbies who were also provided with a kitchen. Thirteen of the green timber-framed shelters survive and are run by the Cabman's Shelter Fund.

**Nearest tube:** Russell Square.

## 10. St Andrew's Square

St Andrew's Gardens is a short walk south from King's Cross St Pancras Station along Gray's Inn Road. It was consecrated in 1754 as a burial ground for St Andrew's Holborn until it was closed in 1885 and converted into public gardens.

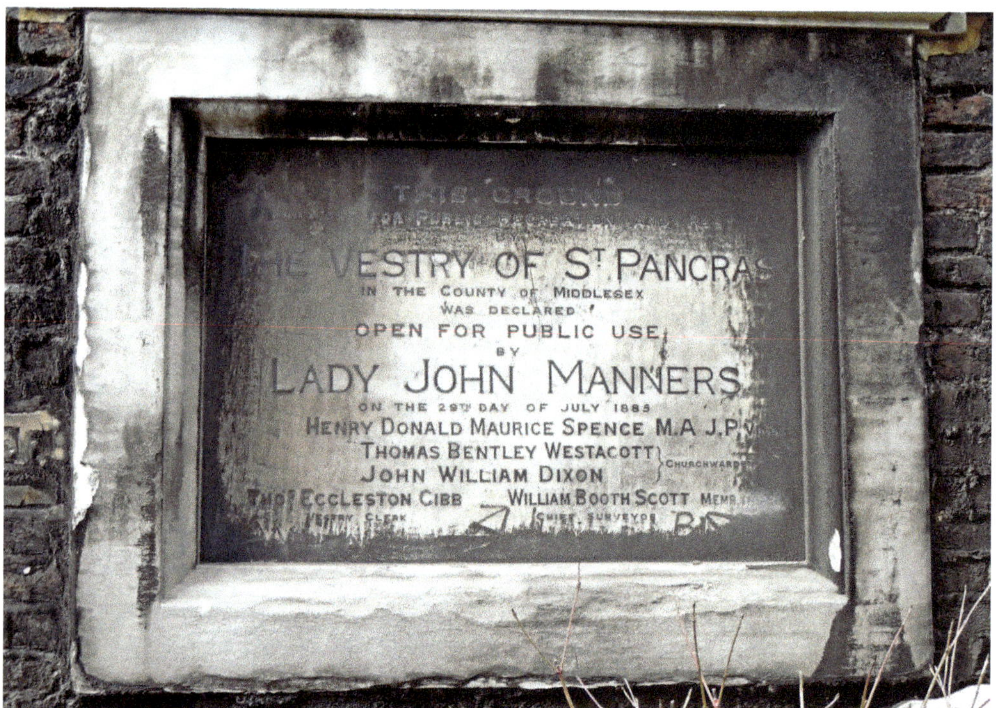


The plaque commemorating the opening of the St Andrew's Gardens in 1885.

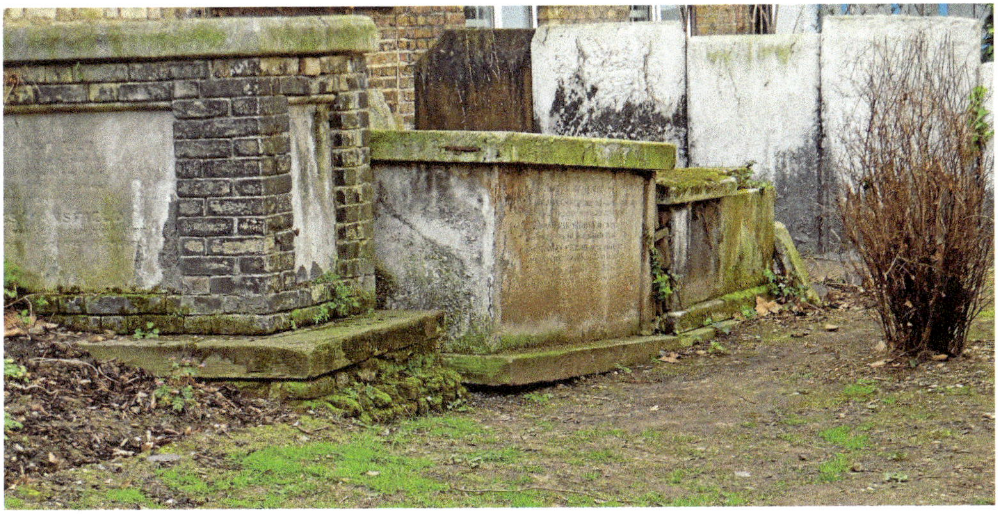

The gravestones in St Andrew's Gardens.

Many headstones bear testimony to the garden's past with most of them resting near the northern entrance where a plaque commemorates the opening of the public garden by Lady Manners on 29 July 1885. There are also a few eighteenth-century tomb chests with weathered inscriptions, one of which dates from 1763.

The gardens are surrounded by nineteenth-century cast-iron railings and are overlooked to the north by Trinity Court, a Modernist block built around 1930. A granite drinking fountain and a small red-brick lodge date from the nineteenth century and are well worth a visit.

**Nearest tube:** King's Cross St Pancras.

## 11. St George's Gardens

St George's Gardens are located south of King's Cross St Pancras Station and well worth a visit. Although a lesser-known square, there is a tranquil atmosphere and much to see in this delightful and secluded place.

The gardens were established in 1713 as a pair of burial grounds to serve the parishes of St George the Martyr, Queen Square and St George's Bloomsbury. They were divided by a brick wall that originally ran along the whole length of the burial grounds, which survives in the western part of the gardens. The gardens were closed to burials in 1854 and reopened as a public garden in 1889. Over time, it became very rundown but received lottery funding and was reopened after extensive restoration work in early 2001.

The two churches of St George were built as part of Queen Anne's programme of providing fifty new churches, paid for by an unpopular tax on coal. Neither church had

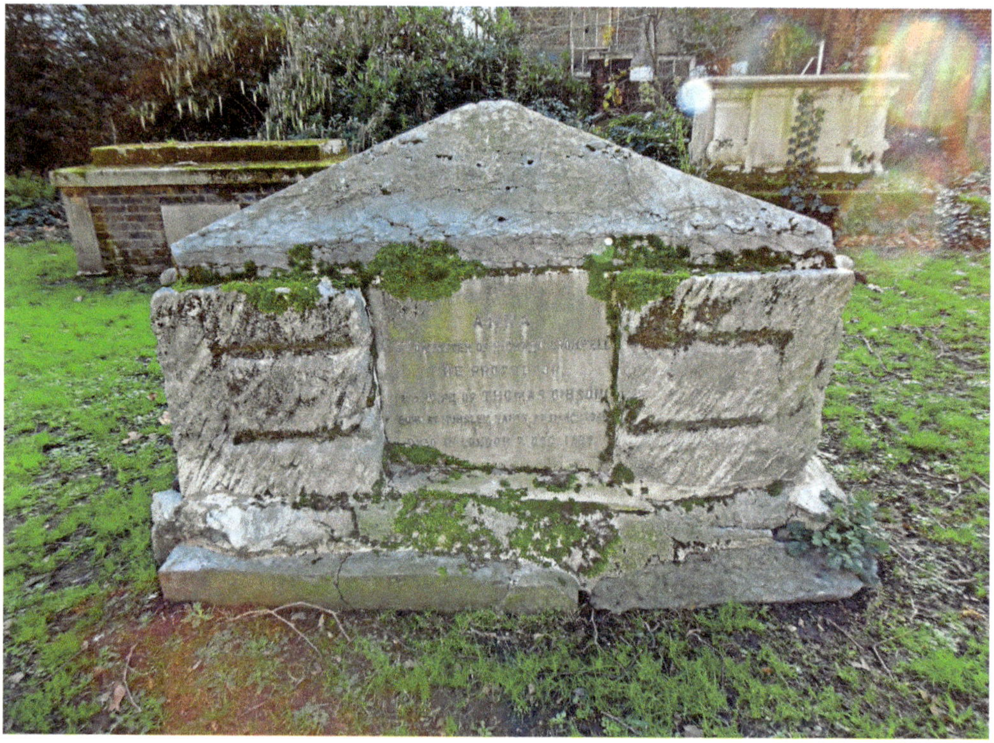

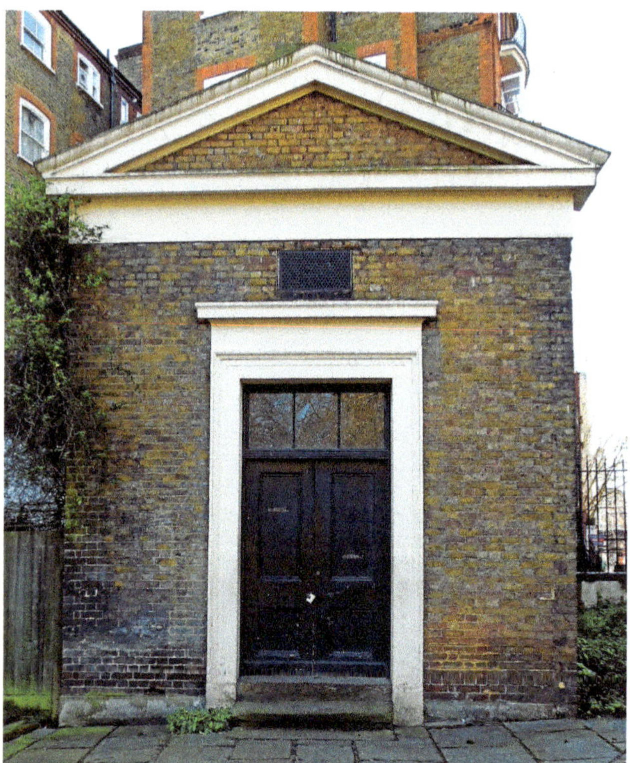

*Above*: The tomb of Anna Gibson, granddaughter of Oliver Cromwell.

*Left*: The Mortuary Chapel in St George's Gardens, built in 1806.

a churchyard but they shared this burial ground, St George using the northern part and St George the Martyr the southern part.

The few monuments and tombs that are still standing represent the hundreds of people who were buried in unmarked graves in this small space. They are also a reminder of the dark history of bodysnatching and it is reputed that the first recorded case took place here.

In a trial heard at Westminster in 1777, the gravediggers John Holmes and Robert Williams were charged with stealing the body of Jane Sainsbury. Williams was stopped while carrying a sack containing the body of a woman. The two men were each sentenced to six months imprisonment and to be 'severely whipped' through the streets. During the eighteenth century, considerable advances in surgery and the scientific study of anatomy were taking place and there was a keen demand for cadavers for teaching, demonstration and dissection purposes, hence the increase in bodysnatching – good specimens could command high prices.

On 30 July 1745, more than a dozen Jacobites were laid to rest in St George's Gardens after being hanged, drawn and quartered on Kennington Common and their headless bodies buried in the gardens. At the western end of the gardens is a mortuary chapel built in 1806, which is now known as the Chapel of Rest.

To the south-east is a memorial to Robert Nelson who died in 1715 and was the first person to be interred there. Since he had designed the layout of the cemetery, it was only right that he reserved the first burial plot for himself. He was noted for charitable work and originally the gardens were known as 'Nelson's Burying Ground'.

An obelisk erected by Thomas Falconer in 1729 and the tomb of Anna Gibson who died in 1726 can be seen at the southern end of the gardens. Anna was the sixth and favourite daughter of Richard Cromwell and granddaughter of Oliver Cromwell.

There is a terracotta statue of the Muse Euterpe. The name means 'delightful' or 'charming' in Greek. Euterpe was one of the Nine Muses, in this case the Muse of Instrumental Music. She was the daughter of Jupiter and Mnemosyne who supposedly invented the double flute and who, like Euterpe, reputedly dispensed joy and pleasure wherever she went. She features in the gardens in the form of a terracotta figure but she looks a trifle lonely. This, perhaps, is not surprising given that she is the only one surviving of eight other carved depictions of the Muses which once adorned the façade of the Apollo pub that stood on the corner of Tottenham Court Road and Torrington Place. When the building was demolished in 1961, this figure was rescued and eventually relocated here.

Along the west wall of the gardens is a fine collection of ferns.

**Nearest tube:** King's Cross St Pancras.

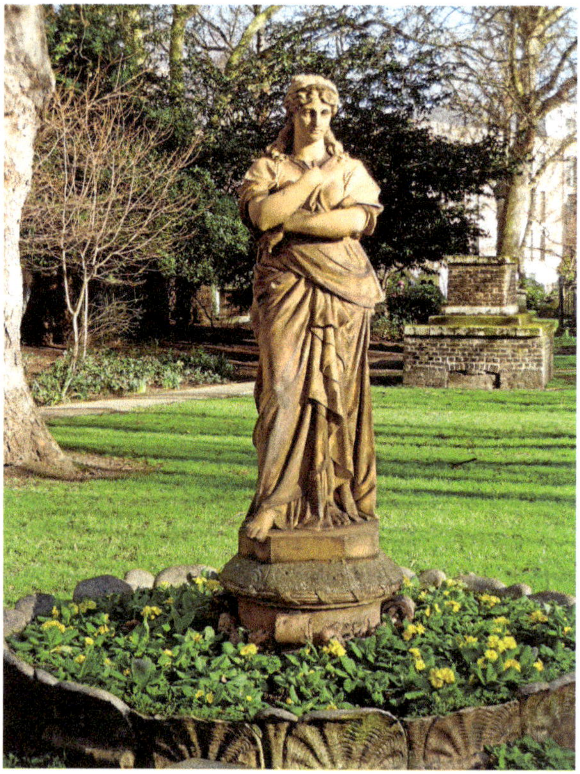

*Left*: A statue of Euterpe, one of the nine Greek muses in St George's Gardens.

*Below*: Gravestones in St George's Gardens.

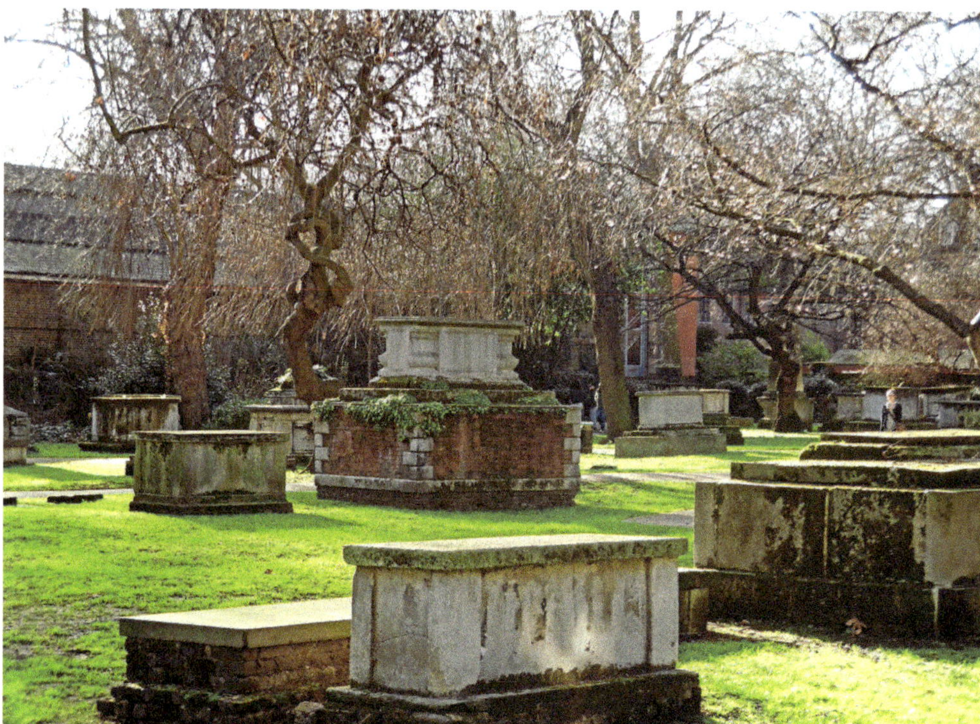

# 12. Tavistock Square

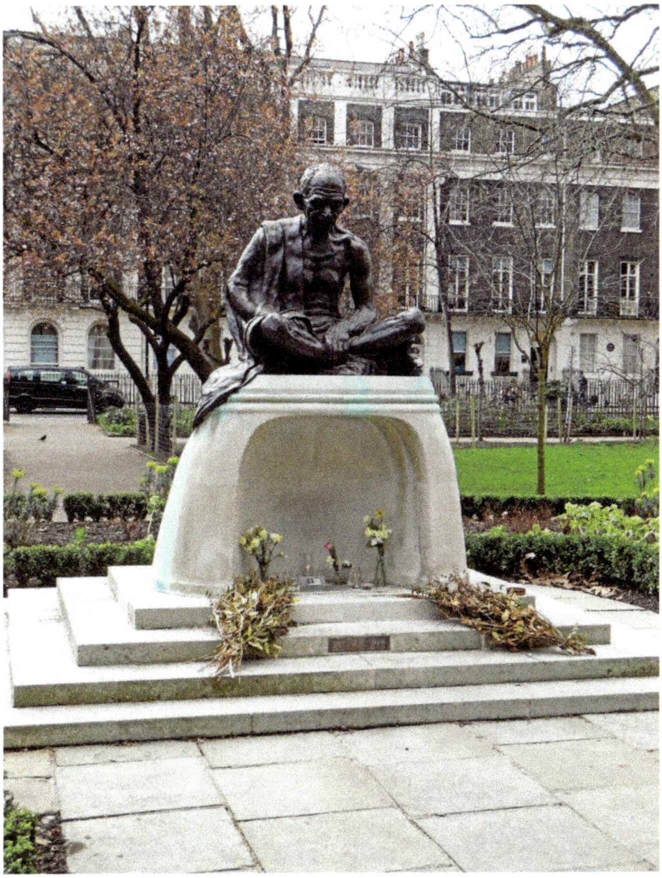

The statue of Gandhi in Tavistock Square.

Tavistock Square lies east of nearby Gordon Square. The first building was started in 1803 and the square was completed in 1826 with the gardens being laid in 1825. Much of the west side consists of the original buildings or at least their original façades. The square is named after the second title of the Dukes of Bedford who are the ground landlords.

The British Medical Association has its headquarters on the eastern side on the site of a house in which Charles Dickens lived from 1851–60. It is thought that he wrote *Bleak House, Hard Times, Little Dorrit* and *A Tale of Two Cities* while resident there. A later tenant disliked this house so much that she published a pamphlet called 'The Ghastly Consequences of Living in Charles Dickens' House'. In the courtyard of the BMA, there is a fountain commemorating medical personnel who died in the Second World War.

At No. 52 lived Leonard and Virginia Woolf. The address became the base for the Hogarth Press, prominent publishers of literature. A Jewish museum can be seen on the north side of the square.

On 7 July 2005 thirteen people were killed on a No. 30 bus as the result of an explosion caused by a suicide bomber. Ironically, the bus had been diverted from its normal route because of earlier terrorist-connected incidents. The explosion occurred close to the BMA building and, fortunately, if that is the right word, people from the building were close at hand to tend to the injured.

The gardens are open and have become something of a sanctuary for those praying for peace. There is a statue of Mahatma Gandhi unveiled by Harold Wilson and a copper beech planted by Nehru in 1955. A cherry tree, planted in 1967, remembers the victims of Hiroshima. A memorial in volcanic slate to Britain's wartime conscientious objectors was unveiled in 1994 by the composer Michael Tibbett. The gardens are sometimes referred to as 'Peace Park'.

**Nearest tube:** Russell Square, Euston.

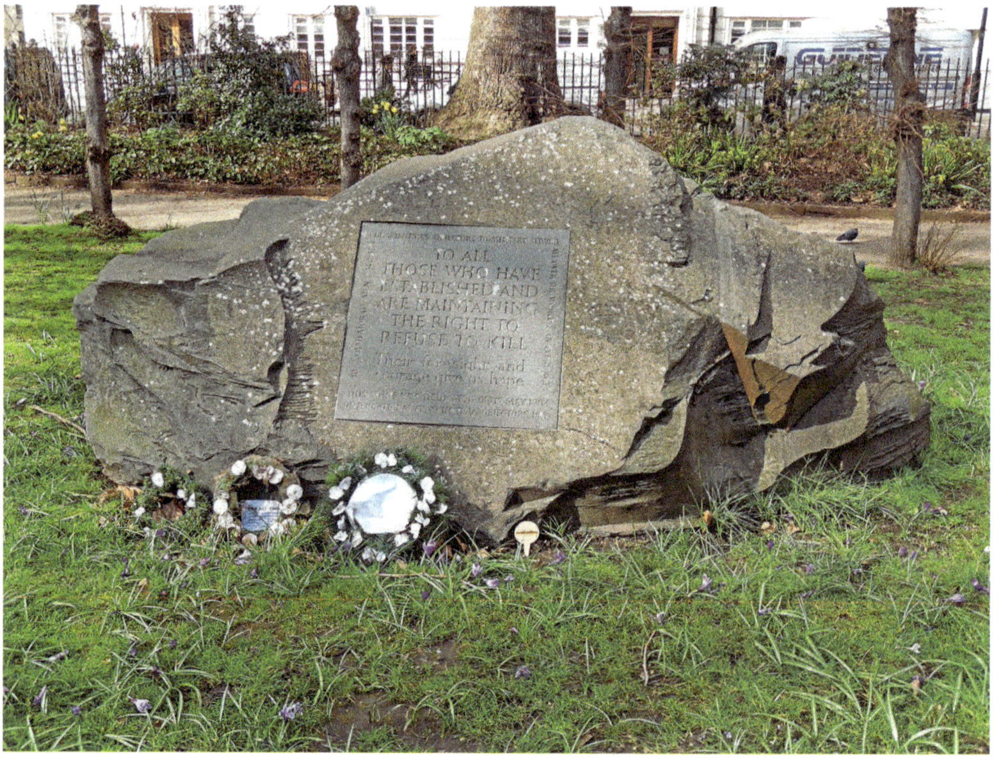


Conscientious objectors commemorative stone, Tavistock Square.